EVE

I WILL GO   .. THEE

AND BE THY GUIDE,

IN THY MOST NEED

TO GO BY THY SIDE

EVERYMAN'S LIBRARY
POCKET POETS

POEMS OF
HEALING

••••••••••••••••••

EDITED BY
KARL KIRCHWEY

EVERYMAN'S LIBRARY
POCKET POETS

Alfred A. Knopf New York London Toronto

THIS IS A BORZOI BOOK
PUBLISHED BY ALFRED A. KNOPF

This selection by Karl Kirchwey
first published in Everyman's Library, 2021
Copyright © 2021 by Everyman's Library

A list of acknowledgments to copyright owners appears
at the back of this volume.

All rights reserved. Published in the United States by Alfred A.
Knopf, a division of Penguin Random House LLC, New York, and
in Canada by Penguin Random House Canada Limited, Toronto.
Distributed by Penguin Random House LLC, New York. Published
in the United Kingdom by Everyman's Library, 50 Albemarle
Street, London W1S 4BD and distributed by Penguin Random
House UK, 20 Vauxhall Bridge Road, London SW1V 2SA.

www.randomhouse/everymans
www.everymanslibrary.co.uk

ISBN 978-1-101-90825-9 (US)
978-1-84159-822-2 (UK)

A CIP catalogue record for this book is available
from the British Library

Typography by Peter B. Willberg

Typeset in the UK by Input Data Services Ltd, Isle Abbotts, Somerset

Printed and bound in Germany
by GGP Media GmbH, Pössneck

CONTENTS

THE DIAGNOSIS

THE HEALING

FOREWORD

"De profundis clamavi," goes the first verse of Psalm 130, "Out of the depths have I cried unto thee, O Lord." Healing is not a final state; it is not an end. It is, instead, a process. Sometimes it begins in those depths, whether they are physical, mental, or spiritual, and moves toward recovery. Healing takes time: and from this point of view, it would seem to be uniquely unsuited to our moment, which is habituated to re-action, rapid absorption and constant change. Healing does not work this way. It shares with poetry the need for participation in a process, if it is to provide a true cure, a lasting relief. Nor does merely *declaring* a cure necessarily make that cure effective, because poetry works by means of laws as mysterious and yet irrefutable as those of science. In poetry there is the genuine cry and the feigned one, just as in medicine there is the genuine cure and the snake oil, and it is helpful to know the difference between them. As the poet, critic and translator Richard Howard observed long ago in another context, poetry is not a lotion or ointment to be slathered on the outside; it is an inner treatment.

I wrote the preceding paragraph in December 2019, having started to gather the poems for this anthology a year before that. Like everyone else in the age of the internet, I was simultaneously connected and disconnected, knowing and clueless, and was only peripherally aware of what had been happening in Wuhan, China. I had no idea that within three months, the Coronavirus pandemic would begin to infect millions, kill hundreds of thousands, and cause worldwide economic devastation.

My primary care physician is also a scholar of the Vedas. Suffering from what I learned was labyrinthitis, an infection of the inner ear causing vertigo, I asked him why dizziness often results in a feeling of intense nausea. He looked at me and smiled and said, "Medicine is not very good at answering the question *Why?*" I was surprised at this response, from one as wise as he. I thought doctors were scientists. I thought answering the question *Why?* was the essence of any medical diagnosis. But maybe this is partly a matter of focus. In her memoir *Body of Work: Meditations on Mortality from the Human Anatomy Lab*, Christine Montross writes, "At times, in fact at most times, specific knowledge in medicine seems to be better understood than general knowledge." Poets, on the other hand, sometimes use the specifics of the world around them to arrive at a more general knowledge of what it means to be alive.

This anthology tracks a process beginning in illness, moving through a diagnosis (whether or not it answers the question *Why?*) to the identification of a remedy, and the possibility of healing. As the only creatures we know of afflicted with a lifelong knowledge of our own eventual extinction, of course we rejoice in our recovery. That rapture takes its point, however, its texture and its authenticity, from the knowledge of what we have come through. And we are never quite cured of what we know lies ahead.

The earliest poem in this anthology is one by the ancient Greek poet Sappho of Lesbos (and she is describing the symptoms of the sickness called being in love); the most recent, a homey reminiscence by a contemporary poet of a rubber hot water bottle, has not yet appeared in a book. The illnesses catalogued here range from "spleen" to substance abuse, from anorexia to AIDS, from depression and bipolar disorder to cancer. The work gathered under the rubric of *Poems of Healing* necessarily overlaps with poems included in other anthologies: of elegies, for example, or poems chronicling emotional extremes. Poetry has always existed next door to sacred chant and magical incantation, too, and even the echo chamber of our age cannot quite erase the fact that *words have power*. Some poems even borrow the list form of a successful Rx. In many poems, healing is not comfort and time does not heal all. In these poems healing is, instead, perfected remembering.

American poet Elizabeth Bishop's villanelle "One

Art," already widely-enough anthologized not to require inclusion here, concludes with the mordant lines "It's evident/ the art of losing's not too hard to master,/ though it may look like (*Write* it!) like disaster." Her parenthesis contains both defiance, and a challenge. For the poets included in this anthology are indeed determined to *write* their way out of illness, or if this is not possible, then by means of words to achieve at least a clear perspective on their own mortality. This requires resourcefulness and bravery, and not infrequently, the way out lies through the love of another person or the support of a community. If there is a single ingredient indispensable to the process and the work of healing, these poems suggest that it is love.

Karl Kirchwey
May 2020

```
            A
          A B
        A B R
      A B R A
    A B R A C
  A B R A C A
A B R A C A D
A B R A C A D A
A B R A C A D A B
A B R A C A D A B R
A B R A C A D A B R A
```

THE ILLNESS

THE ILLNESS

REALLY

This is really happening this is really
not merely my death drawing closer
but the messy undomesticated sprawl

of thought which all but the most fortunate
have to go through here the indignities
degradations anything that might be left

of self-cultivation swiped away and then
you know it might be this day
when you'll be reduced to the outposts

of mind scattered through the corporeal
self and the facts of the flesh
you can no longer regulate or contain

all loosening turning to pathos and grief
and why is this happening you want to ask
while knowing the answer isn't to be borne

"THE SOUL HAS BANDAGED MOMENTS –"

The Soul has Bandaged moments –
When too appalled to stir –
She feels some ghastly Fright come up
And stop to look at her –

Salute her – with long fingers –
Caress her freezing hair –
Sip, Goblin, from the very lips
The Lover – hovered – o'er –

Unworthy, that a thought so mean
Accost a Theme – so – fair –

The soul has moments of Escape –
When bursting all the doors –
She dances like a Bomb, abroad,
And swings upon the Hours,

As do the Bee – delirious borne –
Long Dungeoned from his Rose –
Touch Liberty – then know no more,
But Noon, and Paradise –

The Soul's retaken moments –
When, Felon led along,
With shackles on the plumed feet,
And staples, in the Song,

The Horror welcomes her, again,
These, are not brayed of Tongue –

"THE SICKNESS OF ANGELS IS NOTHING NEW"

The sickness of angels is nothing new.
I have seen them crawling like bees,
Flightless, chewing their tongues, not singing,

Down by the bus terminal, hanging out,
Showing their legs, hiding their wings,
Carrying on for their brief term on earth,

No longer smiling; asleep in the shade of each other
They drift into the arms of strangers who step
Into their light, which is the mascara of Eden,

Offering more than invisible love,
Intangible comforts, offering the taste,
The pure erotic glory of death without echoes,

The feel of kisses blown out of heaven,
Melting the moment they land.

From THE SPLEEN
A Pindaric Poem

What art thou, Spleen, which ev'ry thing dost ape?
   Thou Proteus to abused mankind,
   Who never yet thy real cause could find,
Or fix thee to remain in one continued shape.
   Still varying thy perplexing form,
   Now a Dead Sea thou'lt represent,
   A calm of stupid discontent,
Then, dashing on the rocks wilt rage into a storm.
   Trembling sometimes thou dost appear,
   Dissolved into a panic fear;
   On sleep intruding dost thy shadows spread,
   Thy gloomy terrors round the silent bed,
And crowd with boding dreams the melancholy head;
   Or, when the midnight hour is told,
   And drooping lids thou still dost waking hold,
   Thy fond delusions cheat the eyes,
   Before them antic spectres dance,
Unusual fires their pointed heads advance,
   And airy phantoms rise.

SPLEEN (IV)

When skies are low and heavy as a lid
over the mind tormented by disgust,
and hidden in the gloom the sun pours down
on us a daylight dingier than the dark;

when earth becomes a trickling dungeon where
Trust like a bat keeps lunging through the air,
beating tentative wings along the walls
and bumping its head against the rotten beams;

when rain falls straight from unrelenting clouds,
forging the bars of some enormous jail,
and silent hordes of obscene spiders spin
their webs across the basements of our brains;

then all at once the raging bells break loose,
hurling to heaven their awful caterwaul,
like homeless ghosts with no one left to haunt
whimpering their endless grievances.

– And giant hearses, without dirge or drums,
parade at half-step in my soul, where Hope,
defeated, weeps, and the oppressor Dread
plants his black flag on my assenting skull.

26   CHARLES BAUDELAIRE (1821–67)
     TRANSLATED BY RICHARD HOWARD

LINES WRITTEN DURING A PERIOD OF INSANITY

Hatred and vengeance, my eternal portion,
Scarce can endure delay of execution,
Wait, with impatient readiness, to seize my
           Soul in a moment.

Damned below Judas: more abhorred than he was,
Who for a few pence sold his holy Master.
Twice betrayed Jesus me, the last delinquent,
           Deems the profanest.

Man disavows, and Deity disowns me:
Hell might afford my miseries a shelter;
Therefore hell keeps her ever hungry mouths all
           Bolted against me.

Hard lot! encompassed with a thousand dangers;
Weary, faint, trembling with a thousand terrors;
I'm called, if vanquished, to receive a sentence
           Worse than Abiram's.

Him the vindictive rod of angry justice
Sent quick and howling to the centre headlong;
I, fed with judgment, in a fleshly tomb, am
           Buried above ground.

WILLIAM COWPER (1731–1800)

From HARTFORD

Why do you make me see wrongdoing and look at trouble?
A Puerto Rican mother weeps, her stabbed son intu-
bated before us. Fluorescence illuminates their pietà of
pumps and wires. "Help us, Father," someone says to me
in the confusion of EMTs and doctors administering
CPR. How brave my mother must have been attending
to those about to die. The pink dawn sky bruises the
dilapidated Federalist steeples. They work on the boy
all night long. My mother said: "Do you believe Christ
really rose from the dead? Church every Sunday, don't
you think that's a bit excessive?" When I travel to
Jerusalem, I send a postcard from Yad Vashem. "Dear
Mom," it begins, "I am here." A forgiving snow falls on
the mother and the son. By the end of my shift, I write
in the chart: "The boy died this morning at 6 AM."

THE VIRGIN'S MEMO

maybe not abscesses, acne, asthma,
son, maybe not boils,
maybe not cancer
or diarrhoea
or tinnitus of the inner ear,
maybe not fungus,
maybe rethink the giraffe,
maybe not herpes, son,
or (text illegible)
or jellyfish
or (untranslatable)
maybe not leprosy or lice,
the menopause or mice, mucus, son,
neuralgia, nits,
maybe not body odour,
piles,
quicksand, quagmires,
maybe not rats, son, rabies, rattlesnakes,
shite,
and maybe hang fire on the tarantula,
the unicorn's lovely,
but maybe not veruccas
or wasps,
or (text illegible)
or (untranslatable)
maybe not . . .

CAROL ANN DUFFY (1955 –)   29

From DISENCHANTMENTS
"It is a world, perhaps; but there's another."
  – Edwin Muir

Microbiologizing love, despair,
Delight, bountiful dregs, the pulse can stick
On its heirloom heartbeat. The wear-and-tear

Inherited by who-we-are, echoic
Molecular chronology, begins
At birth. Congenital, genetic,

Against know-nothing, careless inclinations,
Death starts with prophecies half-heard in dreams'
Instinctive narratives. A life's toxins –

Psycho-pollution, maverick spiremes –
Gather like gut-data in the underjoyed
Body's puddles, sponges, muscles, pumps and streams.

All sorts of nastiness lead to the void
On wheels of rotten luck or bad habits,
Cirrhosis, hepatitis B, typhoid,

Mournful *-omas*, murder's vast whodunnits;
Or what we do, or what is done to us,
Those little treacheries, the scolds and frets

Being alive receives from generous
Distributors of selfishness. Over
And over, these can really do for us

As much as age. Competitive disfavour
Churns in the psycho-clock's vascular closet,
Timing private sickness, undercover

Birthday chronometers, almost illicit,
They are so personal; and they contain
Everything, seasons, sky, and the explicit

Derivatives of love, delight, fear, pain,
Betrayals, disappointments. Hereafter
Looks like sacred vision; but it's profane –

God's salesmanship, then His religious laughter.

DOUGLAS DUNN (1942–)   31

[THEY HEAR THE CLAPPING OF THE BELL AND ARE AFRAID]
a song of Lazarus the leper

they hear the clapping of the bell and are afraid
houses untenanted: bedslops spill from the windows
a clump of myrtle.   a scarlet ribbon against the jamb

look to the threshold: house of figs and of affliction
we whom you loved is sick.   maculed and papuled
our extremities knotted and breaking: the cypress
    bends

we was a beautiful lad once: not putrefactive nor foul
not blistering in the lips and nose.   not punctate:
    spots scaling
not mammillated with boils.   nor carbuncled.
    not ulcerated

we also wore purple and byssus: we had carousing
    arms
jeweled and sexy.   required no nurse to dress we
    sores

and we'd easily slake: undeformed, without,
    immaculato

From THE LIGHT-GRAY SOIL

I held him like a passion-tattered cloak.
At four a.m., the hour when one of us
Would turn in sleep to throw a leg across
The other one, protective, unaware,
I knelt, and pressed my forehead to the sheet.
The binding cloth, uncut, undyed, unsewn,
In heaven above, but gathered in my hand.
The end prepared before the sight of all.
A nurse, touching my shoulder: he passed away.
I sought his face: the truthful countenance,

Inviolate stronghold, refuge and redoubt.
Facing extinction in a mental mirror.
The still-unbroken substratum of wonder.
The *mutual flame from hence.* The blowing out.

Forever rest. His head sunk to his chest,
As if he bowed his head at last before
The helpless deed that we were summoned to.
Forever, ever rest. His hand in mine,
Possessive of my hand. All he possessed.
And when I drew my hand away from his,
His hand lay open, certain I was there.
Let nothing evermore be dear to me.

I stood instinctively to hear the call.
The resident physician, feeling for
The artery. A witness from the staff.
Whispered consolation. Four-fifteen.
The time and date and cause recorded, signed.
I swayed, dead on my feet, among the living,
Then stood away, unbidden. Still his wife.
But couldn't draw one breath on his behalf.
Nor add a single heartbeat to his life.

AMONG ENGLISH VERBS

Among English verbs
to die is oddest in its
eagerness to be *dead*,
immodest in its
haste to be told –
a verb alchemical
in the head:
one speck of its gold
and a whole life's lead.

KAY RYAN (1945 –)

DYING

Nothing to be said about it, and everything –
The change of changes, closer or further away:
The Golden Retriever next door, Gussie, is dead,

Like Sandy, the Cocker Spaniel from three doors
    down
Who died when I was small; and every day
Things that were in my memory fade and die.

Phrases die out: first, everyone forgets
What doornails are; then after certain decades
As a dead metaphor, *"dead as a doornail"* flickers

And fades away. But someone I know is dying –
And though one might say glibly, "everyone is,"
The different pace makes the difference absolute.

The tiny invisible spores in the air we breathe,
That settle harmlessly on our drinking water
And on our skin, happen to come together

With certain conditions on the forest floor,
Or even a shady corner of the lawn –
And overnight the fleshy, pale stalks gather,

The colorless growth without a leaf or flower;
And around the stalks, the summer grass keeps
    growing
With steady pressure, like the insistent whiskers

That grow between shaves on a face, the nails
Growing and dying from the toes and fingers
At their own humble pace, oblivious

As the nerveless moths, that live their night or two –
Though like a moth a bright soul keeps on beating,
Bored and impatient in the monster's mouth.

ANOREXIC

Flesh is heretic.
My body is a witch.
I am burning it.

Yes I am torching
her curves and paps and wiles.
They scorch in my self denials.

How she meshed my head
in the half-truths
of her fevers

till I renounced
milk and honey
and the taste of lunch.

I vomited
her hungers.
Now the bitch is burning.

I am starved and curveless.
I am skin and bone.
She has learned her lesson.

Thin as a rib
I turn in sleep.
My dreams probe

a claustrophobia
a sensuous enclosure.
How warm it was and wide

once by a warm drum,
once by the song of his breath
and in his sleeping side.

Only a little more,
only a few more days
sinless, foodless.

I will slip
back into him again
as if I have never been away.

Caged so
I will grow
angular and holy

past pain
keeping his heart
such company

as will make me forget
in a small space
the fall

into forked dark,
into python needs
heaving to hips and breasts
and lips and heat
and sweat and fat and greed.

TALK WITH A HEADACHE

I had this headache. Wherever I went
she followed, though I didn't want

her near me. As a hangover she'd lift
quite quickly. But a stab on the left

would start off a migraine, nausea, the lot
so that my darkened room was lit

by aura explosions. Her red-hot vice
was a cap of neuralgia and she wasn't averse

to a little tinnitus thrown in for fun.
I'd try a broadside of Nurofen

but nothing would shift her, not frozen peas,
nor wormwood. I was on my knees,

begging for mercy. "You've got to see
this is more fun for you than me,

we've got to end it. I'd rather be dead.
I need you like a hole in the head."

She flinched. I felt her draw softly away,
offended. That week was a holiday

from hurting. Now I was free of her throb
I started to act like a total slob,

ate what I liked – kebabs, very late –
watched trash on the telly, was intimate

with dubious women, didn't hear a peep
from the temples she'd left, never rested up.

But there are some things that are worse than pain.
Soon I felt totally put upon

by a zoo of symptoms, was almost dead
with their chattering inside my head

without my guardian. If you see her round
tell her I'm struggling, want to go to ground

with her for a languorous afternoon
away from myself or I'll go insane

for, though she was clothed in a tiresome ache
she cared for me, had a most healthy take

on all my excesses. She was a wife
to me. And I need her knife.

GWYNETH LEWIS (1959–)

TWO TRANSLATIONS OF SAPPHO
FRAGMENT 31

He seems to me equal to gods that man
whoever he is who opposite you
sits and listens close
        to your sweet speaking

and lovely laughing – oh it
puts the heart in my chest on wings
for when I look at you, even a moment, no speaking
        is left in me

no: tongue breaks and thin
fire is racing under skin
and in eyes no sight and drumming
        fills ears

and cold sweat holds me and shaking
grips me all, greener than grass
I am and dead – or almost
        I seem to me.

But all is to be dared, because even a person of
      poverty

       TRANSLATED BY ANNE CARSON

φαίνεταί μοι κῆνος ἴσος θέοισι

Glowing like some god
that man sits so close to you
he tastes your words and the desire
in your laugh,

Just a glance
and my heart pounds me dumb
rips my tongue from silence,
licking

flames spread
beneath my skin, blacking out
my eyes, roaring in my ears,
sweat pours out

sends shivers down
I turn paler than a blade of grass,
I find myself just short
of dying.

THE MAN WITH NIGHT SWEATS

I wake up cold, I who
Prospered through dreams of heat
Wake to their residue,
Sweat, and a clinging sheet.

My flesh was its own shield:
Where it was gashed, it healed.

I grew as I explored
The body I could trust
Even while I adored
The risk that made robust,

A world of wonders in
Each challenge to the skin.

I cannot but be sorry
The given shield was cracked,
My mind reduced to hurry,
My flesh reduced and wrecked.

I have to change the bed,
But catch myself instead

Stopped upright where I am
Hugging my body to me
As if to shield it from
The pains that will go through me,

As if hands were enough
To hold an avalanche off.

THOM GUNN (1929–2004)

THE FUNERAL OF SARPEDON

Zeus mourns deeply:
Patroklos has killed Sarpedon.
Now Patroklos and the Achaians rush forward
to snatch up the body, to dishonor it.

But Zeus does not tolerate that at all.
Though he let his favorite child be killed –
this the Law required –
he will at least honor him after death.
So he now sends Apollo down to the plain
with instructions about how the body should
    be tended.

Apollo reverently raises the hero's body
and carries it in sorrow to the river.
He washes the dust and blood away,
heals its terrible wounds so no trace is left,
pours perfume of ambrosia over it,
and dresses it in radiant Olympian robes.
He bleaches the skin, and with a pearl comb
combs out the jet black hair.
He spreads and arranges the beautiful limbs.

Now he looks like a young king, a royal charioteer –
twenty-five or twenty-six years old –
resting himself after winning
the prize in a famous race,
his chariot all gold and his horses the fastest.

Having finished his task this way,
Apollo calls for the two brothers,
Sleep and Death, and orders them
to take the body to Lykia, the rich country.

So the two brothers, Sleep and Death,
set off on foot toward the rich country, Lykia;
and when they reached the door
of the king's palace,
they handed over the honored body
and then returned to their other labors and concerns.

And once the body was received in the palace
the sad burial began, with processions and honors
        and dirges,
with many libations from sacred vessels,
with all pomp and circumstance.
Then skilled workers from the city
and celebrated craftsmen in stone
came to make the tombstone and the tomb.

JOHN ANDERSON

John Anderson, a scholarly gentleman
advancing with his company in the attack
received some bullets through him as he ran.

So his creative brain whirled, and he fell back
in the bloody dust, (it was a fine day there
and warm). Blood turned his tunic black

while past his desperate final stare
the other simple soldiers run
and leave the hero unaware.

Apt epitaph or pun
he could not hit upon, to grace
a scholar's death; he only eyed the sun.

But I think, the last moment of his gaze
beheld the father of gods and men,
Zeus, leaning from heaven as he dies,

whom in his swoon he hears again
summon Apollo in the Homeric tongue:
Descend Phoebus and cleanse the stain

of dark blood from the body of John Anderson.
Give him to Death and Sleep,
who'll bear him as they can

out of the range of darts, to the broad vale
of Lycia; there lay him in a deep
solemn content on some bright dale.

And the brothers, Sleep and Death
lift up John Anderson at his last breath.

PITY

Pity we killed all the monsters. It might have been
A help to ask a sphinx or a centaur,
A siren, a deep-sea triton or some such cross between
Our miserable species and another
What it feels like. Too late now. Goodbye
Creation, we are all going to die.

Our tinnitus is in the five oceans, the air
Spasms with our constant jabber, our shit trails
Eternally in icy space but here we are
Still ignorant beyond our broken fingernails.
All's in the sights of the camera and the gun
But we've no neighbourhood, no conversation.

Dying from the centre, if we still had a rind
Of greenmen, ariels, mermaids, beings that passed
Through into knowledge of some other kind
We might not be killing and dying quite so fast.
We seed our hard selves over the countryside.
Don't play with us. All who did have died.

STARING AT THE SEA ON THE DAY
OF THE DEATH OF ANOTHER

The long body of the water fills its hollow,
slowly rolls upon its side,
and in the swaddlings of the waves,
their shadowed hollows falling forward with the tide,

like folds of Grecian garments molded to cling
around some classic immemorial marble thing,
I see the vanished bodies of friends who have died.

Each form is furled into its hollow,
white in the dark curl,
the sea a mausoleum, with countless shelves,
cradling the prone effigies of our unearthly selves,

some of the hollows empty, long niches in the tide.
One of them is mine
and gliding forward, gaping wide.

MAY SWENSON (1913–89)   53

THE DIAGNOSIS

CLOTHES

You take off, we take off, they take off
coats, jackets, blouses, double-breasted suits,
made of wool, cotton, cotton-polyester,
skirts, shirts, underwear, slacks, slips, socks,
putting, hanging, tossing them across
the backs of chairs, the wings of metal screens;
for now, the doctor says, it's not too bad,
you may get dressed, get rested up, get out of town,
take one in case, at bedtime, after lunch,
show up in a couple of months, next spring, next year;
you see, and you thought, and we were afraid that,
and he imagined, and you all believed;
it's time to tie, to fasten with shaking hands
shoelaces, buckles, velcro, zippers, snaps,
belts, buttons, cuff links, collars, neckties, clasps
and to pull out of handbags, pockets, sleeves
a crumpled, dotted, flowered, checkered scarf
whose usefulness has suddenly been prolonged.

WISŁAWA SZYMBORSKA (1923–2012)   57
TRANSLATED BY STANISŁAW BARAŃCZAK
AND CLARE CAVANAGH

MISS GEE

Let me tell you a little story
   About Miss Edith Gee;
She lived in Clevedon Terrace
   At Number 83.

She'd a slight squint in her left eye,
   Her lips they were thin and small,
She had narrow sloping shoulders
   And she had no bust at all.

She'd a velvet hat with trimmings,
   And a dark grey serge costume;
She lived in Clevedon Terrace
   In a small bed-sitting room.

She'd a purple mac for wet days,
   A green umbrella too to take,
She'd a bicycle with shopping basket
   And a harsh back-pedal brake.

The Church of Saint Aloysius
   Was not so very far;
She did a lot of knitting,
   Knitting for that Church Bazaar.

Miss Gee looked up at the starlight
    And said, "Does anyone care
That I live in Clevedon Terrace
    On one hundred pounds a year?"

She dreamed a dream one evening
    That she was the Queen of France
And the Vicar of Saint Aloysius
    Asked Her Majesty to dance.

But a storm blew down the palace,
    She was biking through a field of corn,
And a bull with the face of the Vicar
    Was charging with lowered horn.

She could feel his hot breath behind her,
    He was going to overtake;
And the bicycle went slower and slower
    Because of that back-pedal brake.

Summer made the trees a picture,
    Winter made them a wreck;
She bicycled to the evening service
    With her clothes buttoned up to her neck.

She passed by the loving couples,
    She turned her head away;
She passed by the loving couples
    And they didn't ask her to stay.

Miss Gee sat down in the side-aisle,
    She heard the organ play;
And the choir it sang so sweetly
    At the ending of the day.

Miss Gee knelt down in the side-aisle,
    She knelt down on her knees;
"Lead me not into temptation
    But make me a good girl, please."

The days and nights went by her
    Like waves round a Cornish wreck;
She bicycled down to the doctor
    With her clothes buttoned up to her neck.

She bicycled down to the doctor,
    And rang the surgery bell;
"O, doctor, I've a pain inside me,
    And I don't feel very well."

Doctor Thomas looked her over,
    And then he looked some more;
Walked over to his wash-basin,
    Said, "Why didn't you come before?"

Doctor Thomas sat over his dinner,
    Though his wife was waiting to ring,
Rolling his bread into pellets;
    Said, "Cancer's a funny thing.

"Nobody knows what the cause is,
    Though some pretend they do;
It's like some hidden assassin
    Waiting to strike at you.

"Childless women get it,
    And men when they retire;
It's as if there had to be some outlet
    For their foiled creative fire."

His wife she rang for the servant,
    Said, "Don't be so morbid, dear";
He said: "I saw Miss Gee this evening
    And she's a goner, I fear."

They took Miss Gee to the hospital,
    She lay there a total wreck,
Lay in the ward for women
    With the bedclothes right up to her neck.

They laid her on the table,
    The students began to laugh;
And Mr Rose the surgeon
    He cut Miss Gee in half.

Mr Rose he turned to his students,
    Said, "Gentlemen, if you please,
We seldom see a sarcoma
    As far advanced as this."

They took her off the table,
    They wheeled away Miss Gee
Down to another department
    Where they study Anatomy.

They hung her from the ceiling,
    Yes, they hung up Miss Gee;
And a couple of Oxford Groupers
    Carefully dissected her knee.

LITTLE COMPTON

Young Doctor von Trapp
of the singing von Trapps
aimed at my knee with the reflex hammer,
its rubber head a pink triangle of gum.
The leg leapt forward on its own.
They also called it a tomahawk hammer.

DECISION TREE

More root than branch, each choice
a finger sunk into darker soil,
the mole-blind groping pathways
slowly uprooting all that's real.

A chill of knives or burning rays,
hormonal or chemical variations;
burst to sink node, chance to end
& all the countless permutations.

The curve & coefficient of risk,
utility function & influence:
anemic tendrils push against
the porous world of fact & sense.

Possibles, probables, freaks of fate,
one in a thousand, one ninety-ninth;
your options run from left to right,
your fear has the run of a labyrinth.

ANTIDOTE

The virus replicates inside the cell.
The virus cannot live without its host.
The virus hides. The virus kills its host,
But not before it spreads into the cells
Of someone else, another host. It kills
That which it needs to live. It hides
Inside a cell. I have no place to hide:
I'm the host the virus wants to kill.
You see, the killing virus has no soul.
The virus cannot live without my life.
The virus replicates. It needs my life
To live, but it can never have my soul.
The soulless, killing virus replicates
Inside my cells. I am its host. I die
By cells each day. I know, the more I die,
It's me the virus never replicates.

SONNET: INTERMITTENT CLAUDICATION

I told a doctor, at a party, all about how
I kicked a football in a dream and next day
my left knee was strained and extremely painful
and how I walked about 5½ miles to a bookshop in
    Toronto
and the calf of my left leg gave up.
It comes and goes, I said.

What you have, an effect of old age, he said,
is called intermittent claudication.
You remember the lameness of the Emperor Claudius?

But what I remembered was the medical report on
    Yeats:
We have here an agèd arteriosclerotic (was his doctor
    Gogarty?)
and how Yeats said he would rather be called an agèd
    arteriosclerotic
than King of Lower Egypt.

Ah, the words! The words! They can reconcile us to
    anything!

PROGNOSIS

I walked alone in the chill of dawn
while my mind leapt, as the teachers

of detachment say, like a drunken
monkey. Then a gray shape, an owl,

passed overhead. An owl is not
like a crow. A crow makes convivial

chuckings as it flies,
but the owl flew well beyond me

before I heard it coming, and when it
settled, the bough did not sway.

JANE KENYON (1947–95)   67

CANCER

the first time the dreaded word
bangs against your eyes so that
you think you must have heard it but
what you know is that the room
is twisting crimson on its hinge
and all the other people there are dolls
watching from their dollhouse chairs

the second time you hear a swoosh as if
your heart has fallen down a well
and shivers in the water there
trying to not drown

the third time and you are so tired
so tired and you nod your head
and smile and walk away from
the angel uniforms the blood
machines and you enter the nearest
movie house and stand in the last aisle
staring at the screen with your living eyes

1994

i was leaving my fifty-eighth year
when a thumb of ice
stamped itself near my heart

you have your own story
you know about the fear the tears
the scar of disbelief

you know the saddest lies
are the ones we tell ourselves
you know how dangerous it is

to be born with breasts
you know how dangerous it is
to wear dark skin

i was leaving my fifty-eighth year
when i woke into the winter
of a cold and mortal body

thin icicles hanging off
the one mad nipple weeping

have we not been good children
did we not inherit the earth

but you must know all about this
from your own shivering life

DIAGNOSIS

The sympathetic young woman doctor
informs me with an awkward uncharacteristic
formality that the laboratory has reported

not only on my blood but on the day's worth
of urine I'd amassed in a plastic bottle and
that I've been *diagnosed* awful word and that

I'm afflicted with a malady the name of which
I've never heard but which arrives now
in an alliterated appellation that sounds to me

utterly harmless what menace after all can
blameless alliteration contain and perhaps
that's why I find myself in spite of myself

blurting out *well that certainly makes things
interesting no?* that's what in my utter
witlessness came blurting *interesting no?*

MEDICAL HISTORY

I've been pregnant. I've had sex with a man
who's had sex with men. I can't sleep.
My mother has, my mother's mother had,
asthma. My father had a stroke. My father's
mother has high blood pressure.
Both grandfathers died from diabetes.
I drink. I don't smoke. Xanax for flying.
Propranolol for anxiety. My eyes are bad.
I'm spooked by wind. Cousin Lilly died
from an aneurysm. Aunt Hilda, a heart attack.
Uncle Ken, wise as he was, was hit
by a car as if to disprove whatever theory
toward which I write. And, I understand,
the stars in the sky are already dead.

MY MAMMOGRAM

I

In the shower, at the shaving mirror or beach,
For years I'd led . . . the unexamined life?
When all along and so easily within reach
(Closer even than the nonexistent wife)

Lay the trouble – naturally enough
Lurking in a useless, overlooked
Mass of fat and old newspaper stuff
About matters I regularly mistook

As a horror story for the opposite sex,
Nothing to do with what at my downtown gym
Are furtively ogled as The Guy's Pecs.

But one side is swollen, the too tender skin
Discolored. So the doctor orders an X-
Ray, and nervously frowns at my nervous grin.

II

Mammography's on the basement floor.
The nurse has an executioner's gentle eyes.
I start to unbutton my shirt. She shuts the door.
Fifty, male, already embarrassed by the size

Of my "breasts," I'm told to put the left one
Up on a smudged, cold, Plexiglas shelf,
Part of a robot half menacing, half glum,
Like a three-dimensional model of the Freudian self.

Angles are calculated. The computer beeps.
Saucers close on a flatness further compressed.
There's an ache near the heart neither dull nor sharp.

The room gets lethal. Casually the nurse retreats
Behind her shield. Anxiety as blithely suggests
I joke about a snapshot for my Christmas card.

III
"No sign of cancer," the radiologist swans
In to say – with just a hint in his tone
That he's done me a personal favor – whereupon
His look darkens. "But what these pictures show . . .

Here, look, you'll notice the gland on the left's
Enlarged. See?" I see an aerial shot
Of Iraq, and nod. "We'll need further tests,
Of course, but I'd bet that what *you've* got

Is a liver problem. Trouble with your estrogen
Levels. It's time, my friend, to take stock.
It happens more often than you'd think to men."

Reeling from its millionth scotch on the rocks,
In other words, my liver's sensed the end.
Why does it come as something less than a shock?

IV
The end of life as I've known it, that is to say —
Testosterone sported like a power tie,
The matching set of drives and dreads that may
Now soon be plumped to whatever new designs

My apparently resentful, androgynous
Inner life has on me. Blind seer?
The Bearded Lady in some provincial circus?
Something that others both desire and fear.

Still, doesn't everyone *long* to be changed,
Transformed to, no matter, a higher or lower state,
To know the leathery D-Day hero's strange

Detachment, the queen bee's dreamy loll?
Yes, but the future each of us blankly awaits
Was long ago written on the genetic wall.

V

So suppose the breasts fill out until I look
Like my own mother . . . ready to nurse a son,
A version of myself, the infant understood
In the end as the way my own death had come.

Or will I in a decade be back here again,
The diagnosis this time not freakish but fatal?
The changes in one's later years all tend,
Until the last one, toward the farcical,

Each of us slowly turned into something that hurts,
Someone we no longer recognize.
If soul is the final shape I shall assume,

The shadow brightening against the fluorescent
    gloom,
An absence as clumsily slipped into as this shirt,
Then which of my bodies will have been the best
    disguise?

POWER

Living   in the earth-deposits   of our history

Today a backhoe divulged   out of a crumbling flank
        of earth
one bottle   amber   perfect   a hundred-year-old
cure for fever   or melancholy   a tonic
for living on this earth   in the winters of this climate

Today I was reading about Marie Curie:
she must have known she suffered   from radiation
        sickness
her body bombarded for years   by the element
she had purified
It seems she denied to the end
the source of the cataracts on her eyes
the cracked and suppurating skin   of her finger-ends
till she could no longer hold   a test-tube or a pencil

She died   a famous woman   denying
her wounds
denying
her wounds   came   from the same source as her
        power

UNDER THE EYES

Its retributions work like clockwork
Along murdering miles of terrace-houses
Where someone is saying, "I am angry,
I am frightened, I am justified.
Every favour, I must repay with interest,
Any slight against myself, the least slip,
Must be balanced out by an exact revenge."

The city is built on mud and wrath.
Its weather is predicted; its streetlamps
Light up in the glowering, crowded evenings.
Time-switches, ripped from them, are clamped
To sticks of sweet, sweating explosive.
All the machinery of a state
Is a set of scales that squeezes out blood.

Memory is just, too. A complete system
Nothing can surprise. The dead are recalled
From schoolroom afternoons, the hill quarries
Echoing blasts over the secured city;
Or, in a private house, a Judge
Shot in his hallway before his daughter
By a boy who shut his eyes as his hand tightened.

A rain of turds; a pair of eyes; the sky and tears.

78 TOM PAULIN (1949–)

"ARE WE ALL ILL WITH ACUTE LONELINESS"

Are we all ill with acute loneliness,
chronic patients trying to recover
the will to love? Yet all we've suffered
from others and ourselves, all the losses
of faith in the human face – when we glimpsed
the animal in the mother's grimace
or in the lover's grin as he promised
the promise no one can keep – made us lapse
back into our separateness. We all feel
absence like a wound. Sometimes the love
of another wounded one acts like a salve
which soothes the dying self but cannot heal
our lives. And perhaps this is what it feels
like to be human, and we are all well?

JULIA ALVAREZ (1950–)   79

"A *WOUNDED* DEER – LEAPS HIGHEST –"

A *Wounded* Deer – leaps highest –
I've heard the Hunter tell –
'Tis but the Ecstasy of *death* –
And then the Brake is still!

The *Smitten* Rock that gushes!
The *trampled* Steel that springs!
A Cheek is always redder
Just where the Hectic stings!

Mirth is the Mail of Anguish –
In which it Cautious Arm,
Lest anybody spy the blood
And "you're hurt" exclaim!

THE REMEDY

THE REMEDY

ABC

Any body can die, evidently. Few
Go happily, irradiating joy,

Knowledge, love. Many
Need oblivion, painkillers,
Quickest respite.

Sweet time unafflicted,
Various world:

X = your zenith.

ROBERT PINSKY (1940–)

BEFORE THE GAME

Shut one eye then the other
Peek into every corner of yourself
See that there are no nails no thieves
See that there are no cuckoo's eggs

Shut then the other eye
Squat and jump
Jump high high high
On top of yourself

Fall then with all your weight
Fall for days on end deep deep deep
To the bottom of your abyss

Who doesn't break into pieces
Who remains whole who gets up whole
Plays

TRANSLATED BY CHARLES SIMIC

AFTER THE GAME

Finally the hands grab the belly
So the belly won't burst with laughter
Only there's no belly

One hand barely lifts itself
To wipe the cold sweat from its forehead
There's no forehead either

The other hand reaches for the heart
So the heart won't leap out of the chest
But there's no heart either

Both hands fall
They fall idly into the lap
There's no lap either

In the palm of one hand
Now the rain falls
From the other the grass grows
What can I tell you

VASKO POPA (1922–91)
TRANSLATED BY CHARLES SIMIC

EIGHT HAIKU

again and again
I asked, how deep
is the snow?

how much longer
do I have to live?
short summer night

I talk to myself
and hug a hot water bottle
no longer hot ·

cask-mellowed persimmon
held aloft by one hand and
sketched with the other

for the invalid
a gift of sea bream
on a rainy day in May

crank up that wind machine
until these potted flowers
fall off and scatter

if anyone asks,
I'm still alive!
autumn winds

like a little snail
raising his head
for a look around

MASAOKA SHIKI (1867–1902)
TRANSLATED BY J. KEITH VINCENT

BREVIARY

Lord,
   I give thanks to You for this whole jumble of life
   in which I have been drowning helplessly from
   time immemorial, dead set on a constant search
   for trifles.

   Praise be to You, that you gave me unobtrusive
   buttons, pins, suspenders, spectacles, ink streams,
   ever hospitable blank sheets of paper, transparent
   covers, folders patiently waiting.

   Lord, I give thanks to You for syringes with
   needles thick and hair-thin, bandages, every kind
   of Band-aid, the humble compress, thank you for
   the drip, for saline solutions, tubes and above all
   for sleeping pills with names like Roman nymphs,

   which are good, for they invite, imitate, substitute
   for death.

88   ZBIGNIEW HERBERT (1924–98)
     TRANSLATED BY ALISSA VALLES

From DE MEDICAMENTIS

So consult doctors carefully according to situation

And illness and condition at that age,

Whether you prefer to present a cure to a sick person
    with herbs

Or with a spell: for a spell is a sure thing for health,

Bestowing miracles from mysterious words.

What philosophers of nature have discovered for
    human cures,

And what Nature has brought forth by her bounty on
    land and sea,

She, Nature, gives birth to these things, at once
    nourisher and creator

of all kinds of offspring. And so she supplies health-
    bringing cures

in abundance, created from sea and from earth,

from snake, beast, herd and crop, bird, oyster, fish,

milk, wine, fruit, liquid, salt, honey and olive,

juices, nails, pine, pitch, sulfur, wax,

dust, spelt, beans, flax, sawdust, wool, horn,

berries and nuts, timber, coal, ash,

flowers and various herbs, vegetables and metals,

vermilion and chalk, white lead, pumice, gypsum,

calamine, rock alum, flower of copper, molted copper,

soft tin, flake of copper, copper and blackening dye.

Add also – whether you pound it first or beat it in a
    circle –

the fresh produce of the garden, or the dried of the
    larder,

the herbs garlic and thyme, and health-bringing
    savory,

cabbage and radishes and endives with long stems,

and mint and mustard, and sprouts of coriander,

rocket and parsley, mallows and health-bringing beet,

rue and cress and bitter wormwood: mix them,

and powerful pennyroyal, and not without delicate
    cumin.

Whoever reads this, you will be able to decide for
    yourself

whether these things should be understood, or
    actually carried out.

Yet whoever decides upon this area of study, I ask you:

Come to it with pure judgment and a well-wishing
    mind.

Thus may your limbs grow with everlasting strength,

And may you live out a quiet life through many
    decades.

Thus may you cast no aspersions on a strong and
    quiet old age,

And let you never have any need for doctors, and let
    no accident

or disease ever bring forth any pain for you,

but may you live far from troubles and with a sound
    body,

and may your life have as many years as this poem has
    verses.

92 MARCELLUS EMPIRICUS (*fl. c.* 395 CE)
    TRANSLATED BY JAMES UDEN

From HAVING IT OUT WITH MELANCHOLY

> *If many remedies are prescribed for an illness,*
> *you may be certain that the illness has no cure.*
>
> A. P. CHEKHOV
The Cherry Orchard

BOTTLES

Elavil, Ludiomil, Doxepin,
Norpramin, Prozac, Lithium, Xanax,
Wellbutrin, Parnate, Nardil, Zoloft.
The coated ones smell sweet or have
no smell; the powdery ones smell
like the chemistry lab at school
that made me hold my breath.

SUGGESTION FROM A FRIEND

You wouldn't be so depressed
if you really believed in God.

OFTEN

Often I go to bed as soon after dinner
as seems adult
(I mean I try to wait for dark)
in order to push away

from the massive pain in sleep's
frail wicker coracle.

IN AND OUT

The dog searches until he finds me
upstairs, lies down with a clatter
of elbows, puts his head on my foot.

Sometimes the sound of his breathing
saves my life – in and out, in
and out; a pause, a long sigh. . . .

PARDON

A piece of burned meat
wears my clothes, speaks
in my voice, dispatches obligations
haltingly, or not at all.
It is tired of trying
to be stouthearted, tired
beyond measure.

We move on to the monoamine
oxidase inhibitors. Day and night
I feel as if I had drunk six cups
of coffee, but the pain stops
abruptly. With the wonder
and bitterness of someone pardoned

for a crime she did not commit
I come back to marriage and friends,
to pink-fringed hollyhocks; come back
to my desk, books, and chair.

WOOD THRUSH
High on Nardil and June light
I wake at four,
waiting greedily for the first
notes of the wood thrush. Easeful air
presses through the screen
with the wild, complex song
of the bird, and I am overcome

by ordinary contentment.
What hurt me so terribly
all my life until this moment?
How I love the small, swiftly
beating heart of the bird
singing in the great maples;
its bright, unequivocal eye.

MELANCHOLY OF JASON KLEANDER, POET IN KOMMAGINI, AD 595

The aging of my body and my beauty
is a wound from a merciless knife.
I'm not resigned to it at all.
I turn to you, Art of Poetry,
because you have a kind of knowledge about drugs:
attempts to numb the pain, in Imagination and
      Language.

It is a wound from a merciless knife.
Bring your drugs, Art of Poetry –
they numb the wound at least for a little while.

C. P. CAVAFY (1863–1933)
TRANSLATED BY EDMUND KEELEY AND
PHILIP SHERRARD

THE FLOWER THAT DROPS ITS PETALS

I will not die from absence.
A hummingbird pinched the eye of my flower
and my heart mourns and shivers,
does not breathe.
My wings tremble like the long-billed curlew
when he foretells the sun and the rain.
I will not die from absence, I tell myself.
A melody bows down upon the throne of my sadness,
an ocean springs from my stone of origin.
I write in Zapotec to ignore the syntax of pain,
ask the sky and its fire
to give me back my happiness.
Paper butterfly that sustains me:
why did you turn your back upon the star
that knotted your navel?

NATALIA TOLEDO (1968–)   97
TRANSLATED BY CLARE SULLIVAN

"ALTHOUGH A POEM ARISES ..."

Although a poem arises when there's nothing else
to be done, although a poem is a last attempt at order
when one can't stand the disorder any longer,

   although poets are most needed when freedom,
vitamin C, communications, laws and hypertension
therapy are also most needed,

   although to be an artist is to fail and art is fidelity to
failure, as Samuel Beckett says,

   a poem is not one of the last but of the first things
of man.

"ALTHOUGH A POEM IS …"

Although a poem is only a little word machine/ as William Carlos Williams says/ a little word machine ticking in the world of megamachines and megatons and megaelectronvolts,

although in the world of a poem one doesn't live any better than in any other world, although the world of a poem is dreary, arises out of desolation and perishes in the desolation of spiritual history,

although art doesn't solve problems but rather only wears them out, as Susan Sontag says,

yet a poem is the only sword and shield:

for in principle and essence it is not against tyrants, against automobiles, against madness and cancer and the gates of death, but against what is there all the time, all the time inside and out, all the time in front, behind, and in the middle, all the time with us and against us.

It is against emptiness. A poem is being as against emptiness. Against the primary and secondary emptiness.

MIROSLAV HOLUB (1923−98)   99
TRANSLATED BY IAN AND JARMILA MILNER

CALIBRATIONS

She tunes her guitar for Landstuhl
where she will sit on beds and sing
ballads from when Romany
roamed Spain

. . .

A prosthetic hand calibrates perfectly
the stem of a glass
or how to stroke a face
is this how far we have come
to make love easy

Ghost limbs go into spasm in the night
You come back from war with the body you have

. . .

What you can't bear
carry endure lift
you'll have to drag

it'll come with you the ghostlimb

the shadow   blind
echo of your body spectre of your soul

. . .

Let's not talk yet of making love
nor of ingenious devices
replacing touch

And this is not theoretical:
A poem with calipers to hold a heart
so it will want to go on beating

THE GREEN ROOM

Shades of the green room about this scenario.
You lounge beneath the drip of the chemo,
talking shop with others, some bald, some still blest
with their own mops of hair, making the best
of your body's flaw and a visitor's melodrama.
You slip in and out of your latest part: the nausea,
dry mouth, diarrhea, the poison's impact,
having to go back out and face the next act.
The nurse assures you that you look just fine
even in your wig, that you're eternally twenty-nine.
You perk up, introduce "My son, the poet" to
    everyone.
A bald lady asks, "Do your poems rhyme like that
    one –
Fear no more the heat o' the sun – we did in school?
Write us one like that." "Okeydoke," says I, playing
    the fool.

"WHEN AFTER A LONG SILENCE ONE PICKS UP THE PEN"

When after a long silence one picks up the pen
And leans over the paper and says to himself:
Today I shall consider Marsyas

Whose body was flayed to excess,
Who made no crime that would square
With what he was made to suffer.

Today I shall consider the shredded remains of
      Marsyas —
What do they mean as they gather the sunlight
That falls in pieces through the trees,

As in Titian's late painting? Poor Marsyas,
A body, a body of work as it turns and falls
Into suffering, becoming the flesh of light,

Which is fed to onlookers centuries later.
Can this be the cost of encompassing pain?
After a long silence, would I, whose body

Is whole, sheltered, kept in the dark by a mind
That prefers it that way, know what I'd done
And what its worth was? Or is a body scraped

From the bone of experience, the chart of suffering
To be read in such ways that all flesh might be
    redeemed,
At least for the moment, the moment it passes into
    song.

A SLIP OF PAPER

Today I went to the doctor –
the doctor said I was dying,
not in those words, but when I said it
she didn't deny it –

What have you done to your body, her silence says.
We gave it to you and look what you did to it,
how you abused it.
I'm not talking only of cigarettes, she says,
but also of poor diet, of drink.

She's a young woman; the stiff white coat disguises
        her body.
Her hair's pulled back, the little female wisps
suppressed by a dark band. She's not at ease here,

behind her desk, with her diploma over her head,
reading a list of numbers in columns,
some flagged for her attention.
Her spine's straight also, showing no feeling.

No one taught me how to care for my body.
You grow up watched by your mother or
        grandmother.

Once you're free of them, your wife takes over,
      but she's nervous,
she doesn't go too far. So this body I have,
that the doctor blames me for – it's always been
      supervised by women,
and let me tell you, they left a lot out.

The doctor looks at me –
between us, a stack of books and folders.
Except for us, the clinic's empty.

There's a trap-door here, and through that door,
the country of the dead. And the living push you
      through,
they want you there first, ahead of them.

The doctor knows this. She has her books,
I have my cigarettes. Finally
she writes something on a slip of paper.
This will help your blood pressure, she says.

And I pocket it, a sign to go.
And once I'm outside, I tear it up, like a ticket to
      the other world.

She was crazy to come here,
a place where she knows no one.

She's alone; she has no wedding ring.
She goes home alone, to her place outside the village.
And she has her one glass of wine a day,
her dinner that isn't a dinner.

And she takes off that white coat:
between that coat and her body,
there's just a thin layer of cotton.
And at some point, that comes off too.

To get born, your body makes a pact with death,
and from that moment, all it tries to do is cheat —

You get into bed alone. Maybe you sleep, maybe you
        never wake up.
But for a long time you hear every sound.
It's a night like any summer night; the dark never
        comes.

LOUISE GLÜCK (1943–)   107

KLEITOS' ILLNESS

Kleitos, a sympathetic young man,
about twenty-three years of age –
with an excellent upbringing, with rare Greek
    learning –
is critically ill. The fever that decimated
Alexandria this year found him.

Fever found him morally exhausted also,
sick with grief that his companion, a young actor,
had ceased to love him and to desire him.

He is critically ill, and his parents tremble.

And an aged servant who had raised him
also trembles for the life of Kleitos.
In her terrible anxiety
there comes to her mind an idol
she worshipped as a child, before coming here, as a
    servant,
in this house of illustrious Christians, and turning
    Christian.
Secretly she takes some pancakes, some wine and
    honey.
She brings them before the idol. She chants all the
    prayerful

tunes she remembers, beginnings, ends, or middles.
    The idiot
does not understand that the black demon cares little
whether a Christian is cured or is not cured.

C. P. CAVAFY (1863 – 1933)   109
TRANSLATED BY RAE DALVEN

HYMNE TO GOD MY GOD,
IN MY SICKNESSE

Since I am comming to that Holy roome,
   Where, with thy Quire of Saints for evermore,
I shall be made thy Musique; As I come
    I tune the Instrument here at the dore,
    And what I must doe then, thinke here before.

Whilst my Physitians by their love are growne
   Cosmographers, and I their Mapp, who lie
Flat on this bed, that by them may be showne
    That this is my South-west discoverie
    Per fretum febris, by these streights to die,

I joy, that in these straits, I see my West;
   For, though theire currants yeeld returne to none,
What shall my West hurt me? As West and East
    In all flatt Maps (and I am one) are one,
    So death doth touch the Resurrection.

Is the Pacifique Sea my home? Or are
   The Easterne riches? Is *Jerusalem*?
Anyan, and *Magellan*, and *Gibraltare*,
    All streights, and none but streights, are wayes
      to them,
    Whether where *Japhet* dwelt, or *Cham*, or *Sem*.

We thinke that *Paradise* and *Calvarie*,
    Christs Crosse, and *Adams* tree, stood in one place;
Looke Lord, and finde both *Adams* met in me;
    As the first *Adams* sweat surrounds my face,
    May the last *Adams* blood my soule embrace.

So, in his purple wrapp'd receive mee Lord,
    By these his thornes give me his other Crowne;
And as to others soules I preach'd thy word,
    Be this my Text, my Sermon to mine owne,
    Therefore that he may raise the Lord throws down.

JOHN DONNE (1572–1631)   111

From THE SHIP OF DEATH

VII

We are dying, we are dying, so all we can do
is now to be willing to die, and to build the ship
of death to carry the soul on the longest journey.

A little ship, with oars and food
and little dishes, and all accoutrements
fitting and ready for the departing soul.

Now launch the small ship, now as the body dies
and life departs, launch out, the fragile soul
in the fragile ship of courage, the ark of faith
with its store of food and little cooking pans
and change of clothes,
upon the flood's black waste
upon the waters of the end
upon the sea of death, where still we sail
darkly, for we cannot steer, and have no port.

There is no port, there is nowhere to go
only the deepening blackness darkening still
blacker upon the soundless, ungurgling flood
darkness at one with darkness, up and down
and sideways utterly dark, so there is no direction
  any more

and the little ship is there; yet she is gone.
She is not seen, for there is nothing to see her by.
She is gone! gone! and yet
somewhere she is there.
Nowhere!

VIII
And everything is gone, the body is gone
completely under, gone, entirely gone.
The upper darkness is heavy as the lower,
between them the little ship
is gone

It is the end, it is oblivion.

IX
And yet out of eternity a thread
separates itself on the blackness,
a horizontal thread
that fumes a little with pallor upon the dark.

Is it illusion? or does the pallor fume
a little higher?
Ah wait, wait, for there's the dawn,
the cruel dawn of coming back to life
out of oblivion.

Wait, wait, the little ship
drifting, beneath the deathly ashy grey
of a flood-dawn.

Wait, wait! even so, a flush of yellow
and strangely, O chilled wan soul, a flush of rose.

A flush of rose, and the whole thing starts again.

X
The flood subsides, and the body, like a worn sea-shell
emerges strange and lovely.
And the little ship wings home, faltering and lapsing
on the pink flood,
and the frail soul steps out, into the house again
filling the heart with peace.

Swings the heart renewed with peace
even of oblivion.

Oh build your ship of death. Oh build it!
for you will need it.
For the voyage of oblivion awaits you.

THE RAINCOAT

When the doctor suggested surgery
and a brace for all my youngest years,
my parents scrambled to take me
to massage therapy, deep tissue work,
osteopathy, and soon my crooked spine
unspooled a bit, I could breathe again,
and move more in a body unclouded
by pain. My mom would tell me to sing
songs to her the whole forty-five minute
drive to Middle Two Rock Road and forty-
five minutes back from physical therapy.
She'd say, even my voice sounded unfettered
by my spine afterward. So I sang and sang,
because I thought she liked it. I never
asked her what she gave up to drive me,
or how her day was before this chore. Today,
at her age, I was driving myself home from yet
another spine appointment, singing along
to some maudlin but solid song on the radio,
and I saw a mom take her raincoat off
and give it to her young daughter when
a storm took over the afternoon. My god,
I thought, my whole life I've been under her
raincoat thinking it was somehow a marvel
that I never got wet.

HOT WATER BOTTLE

You're so long dead
and the days when you tended
your teenaged daughter go back so far
that the two of us seem
equally prehistoric.

But today for some
reason, or none –
which happens more and more often –
you resurfaced, like that secret
stabbing in the gut
I'd have to endure at school.
I always forgot how bad it was
until another month had passed.
I always forgot I'd need you again
to soothe me, home from the wars at last,
with a cup of tea and the vaguely
vulva-like red rubber
hot water bottle.

You'd make sure the bottle's stopper
was dialed tight as an oven timer.
An electric heating pad
would have done the trick,
but you preferred to be on call
when the scalding bottle cooled;

to shuffle back to the kitchen, unplug
the thing and empty it in the sink
glug glug and start again.

You lived to see the birth
of my first daughter
but not the second.
That time my water broke all at once,
streamed down my legs,
flooded the front of my thin spring skirt
as I stood barefoot on the grass,
happy and afraid.

Somebody left on earth should know
that when I was young
you doted on me.
I'd lie on the couch,
hot water bottle on my flat
abdomen, and watch TV.
A re-run of *The Red Balloon*,
I'm thinking now.
One time I know it was that.
Whenever it was I saw it,
I remember the tug
of wishing I could catch the bobbing
string for the boy
as his red balloon drifted away.

MARY JO SALTER (1954–)   117

A RECEIPT TO CURE THE VAPOURS

Why will Delia thus retire,
    And idly languish life away?
While the sighing crowd admire,
    'Tis too soon for hartshorn tea:

All those dismal looks and fretting
    Cannot Damon's life restore;
Long ago the worms have eat him,
    You can never see him more.

Once again consult your toilette,
    In the glass your face review:
So much weeping soon will spoil it,
    And no spring your charms renew.

I, like you, was born a woman,
    Well I know what vapours mean:
The disease, alas! is common;
    Single, we have all the spleen.

All the morals that they tell us,
    Never cured the sorrow yet:
Chuse, among the pretty fellows,
    One of honour, youth, and wit.

Prithee hear him every morning
    At the least an hour or two;
Once again at night returning –
    I believe the dose will do.

BLOOD AND LIGHT
In memory of Tony Anderson (1981–2015)

> *Photopheresis involves the removal of blood from the*
> *body and separation of its component parts. Red blood*
> *cells are returned to the body; white blood cells are*
> *treated with a photosensitizing substance and then*
> *irradiated with light prior to their return to the body,*
> *where they will convey to other cells the memory of*
> *a programmed rather than a traumatic cell death.*
> *One use of photopheresis is in treating graft versus*
> *host disease, in which the body's immune system turns*
> *against itself.*

You can do it only with a great machine
        fashioned of mental gray
in Mississauga or Raritan,
        something the color of syncope.

First you must separate
        one from the other, mindful
that apparent unlikenesses are not
        the most profound differences of all.

The majority you may reintroduce
        to the place where they usefully dwelled.

But now, by ineffable degrees,
        leaving no consent to withhold,

you must mix with those that remain a quintessence
        activated only by light
as it was divided from darkness once,
        until they yield to it

– or rather, their belief must succumb,
        that they have been under siege
by an oppressor with no name
        serving only death's advantage,

and they transmit to others
        this revision of strife
into a kind of solace,
        and so pass out of life

teaching the stubborn body
        it need no more resist,
inculcating in memory
        an unexpected trust,

the reviled, contested thing
        now carefully handed on,
and imperceptibly, without arguing,
        with only the sublime deception

121

of the light that enables and justifies,
      as it daily walks the scarred earth
in its contest against reflexes
       too deep to be reasoned with.

PAIN FELLOW

You wake into hurt, *deadspace*
drawn in and pushed out; on fire,
every nerve & joint conveys
annihilating news. Climb higher,

tapping each tread on the stairs
with blind wordlets as you rise,
from *mild* to *moderate* & *severe*,
win your morphine like a prize.

Every motion chafes & wounds.
One to ten? the nurse will ask.
The pain fellow is off on rounds.
Try not to breathe until he's back.

He'll talk your pain back to you
like a runaway animal, a child
that turned hateful when it grew
& burnt its rage up running wild.

ALISSA VALLES (1972–)   123

From PHONE MESSAGES ON CALL

III. *Lost his Rx for pain pills. Pls page pt ASAP.*
     Pt in pain.

It's twenty minutes of his history –
the accident that caused his injury

(which by the way was not his fault – both cars
were totaled), bungled surgeries, the scars

they left him with, the rehabilitation
(which he complied with), also meditation,

some chiropractic quack, a bunch of herbs
(did nothing), acupuncture (damaged nerves),

procedures ranging from electric shocks
to needles in the inflamed spinal tracts,

psychiatrists who told him he was fine
(though personality was "borderline,

like that would fucking help") – before he gets
around to asking me for Percocet,

because narcotics are the only thing
that work. It's like an old familiar song,

the pain just like the lover who is lost,
and leaves a soul that begs to be released

but learns that joy is near enough to hell,
that innocence is irreplaceable.

SUPPORT GROUP

For a long time, each day was a bad day.
Truthfully? For *years*, each day was a bad day.

The nights were worse, but she could slide
The deadbolt on the bedroom door, and swallow
An Ambien, or two, to summon sleep.

Thank god she never dreamed about it.

The meetings helped, but it was hard to go
Because the first thing you did was admit
You were *fucked*, and had no power.

Still: It was worse to stay home, sitting on the fear
Like a solitary hen hatching poisoned eggs.

There were a lot of rules and tissues in the room.
The rules were followed. The tissues were
Dispensed to those who wept.

Many wept.

In the rooms, there was infinite suffering.
It had 3 minutes each to describe itself.

A little timer went off, or someone waved
A cardboard clock face in the air. One Suffering
Stopped talking. Then the next Suffering started up.

A lot of suffering in the world, is the first clear thought
Most people have when they come here.

CHEMOTHERAPY

sorry can't leave just yet
two kids so little
still cry when they stub a toe
need help sticking bandaid
can't go right now
got a class reunion
book on reserve
four tickets to Vancouver no refunds

reading up on survivors
card-playing grandma number on her arm
ten-car pileup wheelchair for life
hopeless coma awoke one morning
bone-cracking tumor size of the sun

couldn't help it
teacher made me
said to lay my head on the desk
but everyone else can leave
heavy door slams
not so fast lady

I'll tell you why
for nothing that's why
for the hell of it

some number came up
so what you gonna do huh
just plain spiteful

put my affairs in order
ten notarized final wishes
now my bald skull
lonely breast broken heart
hunch over the muddy curb
in the filthy wind
no place in particular
wait for light to change

From RADIATION DAYS

My first day at the hospital, I was given a PET scan
And injected intravenously with a thick sugar syrup.
Cancer cells – as who does not? – love sweets
And light up when the syrup oozes near them –
Allowing the scan to track where they have clustered,
Where they are heading. For that one moment only
They are still, grateful, joyous.
Or is it me they like? Short-tempered, blunt,
Vain, miserly, revengeful, diabetic me?
They may not light up but they do return.
This is the second time they have taken up residence
In the same part of my body, the one that oversees
Reproduction and elimination, the minimalist's
Methods, though my cancers seem blowsy.
And why me again? Is that "right"?
I mean, morally, morally right – the wrong question
I ask because I was brought up to believe everything
Is either right or wrong. So is cancer "wrong"?
Cells are behaving unnaturally but only because we do
Not know why. In their own way, they are like the man
Who stands beside me day in, night out, his love
And patience undeserved and unfathomable,
Which may, in this instance, be how best to
        understand
Right and wrong, or join the blessing with the curse.

130   J. D. McCLATCHY (1945–2018)

POEM TO MY LITTER

My genes are in mice, and not in the banal way
that Man's old genes are in the Beasts.

My doctors split my tumors up and scattered them
into the bones of twelve mice. We give

the mice poisons I might, in the future, want
for myself. We watch each mouse like a crystal ball.

I wish it was perfect, but sometimes the death we see
doesn't happen when we try it again in my body.

My tumors are old, older than mice can be.
They first grew in my flank a decade ago.

Then they went to my lungs, and down my femurs,
and into the hives in my throat that hatch white cells.

The mice only have a tumor each, in the leg.
Their tumors have never grown up. Uprooted

and moved. Learned to sleep in any bed
the vast body turns down. Before the tumors can
    spread

they bust open the legs of the mice. Who bleed to
    death.
Next time the doctors plan to cut off the legs

in the nick of time so the tumors will spread.
But I still have both my legs. To complicate things
    further,

mouse bodies fight off my tumors. We have to give
the mice AIDS so they'll harbor my genes peacefully.

I want my mice to be just like me. I don't have any
    children.
I named them all Max. First they were Max 1, Max 2,

but now they're all just Max. No playing favorites.
They don't know they're named, of course.

They're like children you've traumatized
and tortured so they won't let you visit.

I hope, Maxes, some good in you is of me.
Even my suffering is good, in part. Sure I swell

with rage, fear – the stuff that makes you see your tail
as a bar on the cage. But then the feelings pass.

And since I do absolutely nothing (my pride, like my
    fur,
all gone) nothing happens to me. And if a whole lot

of nothing happens to you, Maxes, that's peace.
Which is what we want. Trust me.

COME, HEAVY SLEEP

Come, heavy Sleep, the image of true Death
    And close up these my weary weeping eyes
Whose spring of tears doth stop my vital breath,
      And tears my heart with Sorrow's sigh-swoll'n
        cries.
Come and possess my tired thought-worn soul,
That living dies, till thou on me be stole.

Come, shadow of my end, and shape of rest,
    Allied to Death, child to this black-faced Night;
Come thou and charm these rebels in my breast,
    Whose waking fancies doth my mind affright.
O come, sweet Sleep, come or I die for ever;
Come ere my last sleep comes, or come never.

DEATHWORK

Wake when dog whimpers. Prick
Finger. Inject insulin.
    Glue teeth in.
  Smoke cigarette.
    Shudder and fret.
Feed old dog. Write syllabic

On self-pity. Get *Boston Globe*.
Drink coffee. Eat bagel. Read
    At nervous speed.
  Smoke cigarette.
    Never forget
To measure oneself against Job.

Drag out afternoon.
Walk dog. Don't write.
    Turn off light.
  Smoke cigarette
    Watching sun set.
Wait for the fucking moon.

Nuke lasagna. Pace and curse.
For solitude's support
    Drink Taylor's port.
  Smoke cigarette.
      Sleep. Sweat.
Nightmare until dog whimpers.

From THE RUBA'IYAT

Oh you come hot-foot from the spiritual world,
Distracted by the five senses, four elements, six causes
    and seven planets;
Drink wine since you do not know where you're from,
Be happy, you do not know where you will go.

Oh heart since time's passing grieves you
And your pure spirit so unseasonably leaves the body,
Sit on the green, spend a few days in happiness
Before the green grass springs from your dust.

This pot a workman drinks from
Is made from the eyes of a king, the heart of a vazir;
This wine-bowl in a drunkard's palm
Is made from a cheek flushed with wine and a lady's
    lip.

These few odd days of life have passed
Like water down the brook, wind across the desert;
There are two days I have never been plagued with
    regret for,
Yesterday that has gone, tomorrow that will come.

Before you and I did, night and day existed,
The revolving heavens were busy;
Where you set your foot on the face of the ground
Was the pupil of the eye of a sweetheart.

When the conjunctions of matter are working in your
    favour a moment
Go and live happily, you did not choose your lot;
Keep company with men of science since your bodily
    properties
Are a speck of dust joined with a puff of air, a mote
    with a gasp of breath.

INVITATION TO THE VOYAGE

My child, my sister, dream
How sweet all things would seem
Were we in that kind land to live together,
And there love slow and long,
There love and die among
Those scenes that image you, that sumptuous weather.
Drowned suns that glimmer there
Through cloud-dishevelled air
Move me with such a mystery as appears
Within those other skies
Of your treacherous eyes
When I behold them shining through their tears.

There, there is nothing else but grace and measure,
Richness, quietness, and pleasure.

Furniture that wears
The lustre of the years
Softly would glow within our glowing chamber,
Flowers of rarest bloom
Proffering their perfume
Mixed with the vague fragrances of amber;
Gold ceilings would there be,
Mirrors deep as the sea,
The walls all in an Eastern splendor hung –

Nothing but should address
The soul's loneliness,
Speaking her sweet and secret native tongue.

There, there is nothing else but grace and measure,
Richness, quietness, and pleasure.

See, sheltered from the swells
There in the still canals
Those drowsy ships that dream of sailing forth;
It is to satisfy
Your least desire, they ply
Hither through all the waters of the earth.
The sun at close of day
Clothes the fields of hay,
Then the canals, at last the town entire
In hyacinth and gold:
Slowly the land is rolled
Sleepward under a sea of gentle fire.

There, there is nothing else but grace and measure,
Richness, quietness, and pleasure.

UP

You wake up filled with dread.
There seems no reason for it.
Morning light sifts through the window,
there is birdsong,
you can't get out of bed.

It's something about the crumpled sheets
hanging over the edge like jungle
foliage, the terry slippers gaping
their dark pink mouths for your feet,
the unseen breakfast – some of it
in the refrigerator you do not dare
to open – you will not dare to eat.

What prevents you? The future. The future tense,
immense as outer space.
You could get lost there.
No. Nothing so simple. The past, its density
and drowned events pressing you down,
like sea water, like gelatin
filling your lungs instead of air.

Forget all that and let's get up.
Try moving your arm.
Try moving your head.

Pretend the house is on fire
and you must run or burn.
No, that one's useless.
It's never worked before.
Where is it coming from, this echo,
this huge No that surrounds you,
silent as the folds of the yellow
curtains, mute as the cheerful

Mexican bowl with its cargo
of mummified flowers?
(You chose the colours of the sun,
not the dried neutrals of shadow.
God knows you've tried.)

Now here's a good one:
you're lying on your deathbed.
You have one hour to live.
Who is it, exactly, you have needed
all these years to forgive?

AWAY, MELANCHOLY

Away, melancholy,
Away with it, let it go.

Are not the trees green,
The earth as green?
Does not the wind blow,
Fire leap and the rivers flow?
Away melancholy.

The ant is busy
He carrieth his meat,
All things hurry
To be eaten or eat.
Away, melancholy.

Man, too, hurries,
Eats, couples, buries,
He is an animal also
With a hey ho melancholy,
Away with it, let it go.

Man of all creatures
Is superlative
(Away melancholy)
He of all creatures alone

Raiseth a stone
(Away melancholy)
Into the stone, the god
Pours what he knows of good
Calling, good, God.
Away melancholy, let it go.

Speak not to me of tears,
Tyranny, pox, wars,
Saying, Can God
Stone of man's thought, be good?

Say rather it is enough
That the stuffed
Stone of man's good, growing,
By man's called God.
Away, melancholy, let it go.

Man aspires
To good,
To love
Sighs;

Beaten, corrupted, dying
In his own blood lying
Yet heaves up an eye above
Cries, Love, love.

It is his virtue needs explaining,
Not his failing.

Away, melancholy,
Away with it, let it go.

"MY OWN HEART LET ME MORE HAVE PITY ON"

My own heart let me more have pity on; let
Me live to my sad self hereafter kind,
Charitable; not live this tormented mind
With this tormented mind tormenting yet.

I cast for comfort I can no more get
By groping round my comfortless, than blind
Eyes in their dark can day or thirst can find
Thirst's all-in-all in all a world of wet.

Soul, self; come, poor Jackself, I do advise
You, jaded, let be; call off thoughts awhile
Elsewhere; leave comfort root-room; let joy size

At God knows when to God knows what; whose smile
's not wrung, see you; unforeseen times rather – as
     skies
Betweenpie mountains – lights a lovely mile.

THE HEALING

THE HEALING

BLESSING THE BOATS
(*at St Mary's*)

may the tide
that is entering even now
the lip of our understanding
carry you out
beyond the face of fear
may you kiss
the wind then turn from it
certain that it will
love your back   may you
open your eyes to water
water waving forever
and may you in your innocence
sail through this to that

TRY TO PRAISE THE MUTILATED WORLD

Try to praise the mutilated world.
Remember June's long days,
and wild strawberries, drops of rosé wine.
The nettles that methodically overgrow
the abandoned homesteads of exiles.
You must praise the mutilated world.
You watched the stylish yachts and ships;
one of them had a long trip ahead of it,
while salty oblivion awaited others.
You've seen the refugees going nowhere,
you've heard the executioners sing joyfully.
You should praise the mutilated world.
Remember the moments when we were together
in a white room and the curtain fluttered.
Return in thought to the concert where music flared.
You gathered acorns in the park in autumn
and leaves eddied over the earth's scars.
Praise the mutilated world
and the gray feather a thrush lost,
and the gentle light that strays and vanishes
and returns.

    TRANSLATED BY CLARE CAVANAGH

THE END AND THE BEGINNING

After every war
someone has to tidy up.
Things won't pick
themselves up, after all.

Someone has to shove
the rubble to the roadsides
so the carts loaded with corpses
can get by.

Someone has to trudge
through sludge and ashes,
through the sofa springs,
the shards of glass,
the bloody rags.

Someone has to lug the post
to prop the wall,
someone has to glaze the window,
set the door in its frame.

No sound bites, no photo opportunities,
and it takes years.
All the cameras have gone
to other wars.

The bridges need to be rebuilt,
the railroad stations, too.
Shirtsleeves will be rolled
to shreds.

Someone, broom in hand,
still remembers how it was.
Someone else listens, nodding
his unshattered head.

But others are bound to be bustling nearby
who'll find all that
a little boring.

From time to time someone still must
dig up a rusted argument
from underneath a bush
and haul it off to the dump.

Those who knew
what this was all about
must make way for those
who know little.
And less than that.
And at last nothing less than nothing.

Someone has to lie there
in the grass that covers up
the causes and effects
with a cornstalk in his teeth,
gawking at clouds.

WISŁAWA SZYMBORSKA (1923–2012)   153
TRANSLATED BY STANISŁAW BARAŃCZAK
AND CLARE CAVANAGH

ON THE DEATH OF THE AMIR'S FATHER

You who are sad, who suffer,
Who hide your eyes that flow with tears
For him, whose name I don't mention
For fear of more sorrow and hardship:
Went what went and came what came,
Was what was, why grieve in vain?
You want to give harmony to the world?
The world will not accept harmony from you.
Don't complain, it doesn't heed complaints.
Stop wailing, it doesn't hear you wail.
Even if you wail until the day of reckoning,
How can wailing bring back the one who is gone?
You will see more torment from this wheel
If you are tormented at every turn.
It's as if disasters have been assigned
To whomever you give your heart.
There are no clouds, there's no eclipse,
But the moon is covered, the earth is dark.
Accept it or not, I am sorry to say
You will not be able to conquer yourself.
To break the siege of sorrow on your heart
It is better to fetch the wine, and drink.
Out of great disasters, there will appear
Virtue and grace and nobility.

154   RUDAKI (*c.* 880–941)
  TRANSLATED BY SASSAN TABATABAI

SONG
(from *Cymbeline*)

Fear no more the heat o' th' sun,
 Nor the furious winter's rages,
Thou thy worldly task hast done,
 Home art gone and ta'en thy wages.
Golden lads and girls all must,
As chimney-sweepers, come to dust.

Fear no more the frown o' th' great,
 Thou art past the tyrant's stroke,
Care no more to clothe and eat,
 To thee the reed is as the oak:
The sceptre, learning, physic, must
All follow this and come to dust.

Fear no more the lightning-flash,
 Nor th' all-dreaded thunder-stone;
Fear not slander, censure rash;
 Thou hast finish'd joy and moan.
All lovers young, all lovers must
Consign to thee and come to dust.

No exorciser harm thee!
Nor no witchcraft charm thee!

Ghost unlaid forbear thee!
Nothing ill come near thee!
Quiet consummation have,
And renownèd be thy grave!

A REFUSAL TO MOURN THE DEATH, BY FIRE, OF A CHILD IN LONDON

Never until the mankind making
Bird beast and flower
Fathering and all humbling darkness
Tells with silence the last light breaking
And the still hour
Is come of the sea tumbling in harness

And I must enter again the round
Zion of the water bead
And the synagogue of the ear of corn
Shall I let pray the shadow of a sound
Or sow my salt seed
In the least valley of sackcloth to mourn

The majesty and burning of the child's death.
I shall not murder
The mankind of her going with a grave truth
Nor blaspheme down the stations of the breath
With any further
Elegy of innocence and youth.

Deep with the first dead lies London's daughter,
Robed in the long friends,
The grains beyond age, the dark veins of her mother,
Secret by the unmourning water
Of the riding Thames.
After the first death, there is no other.

QUARANTINE

(from *Marriage*)

In the worst hour of the worst season
    of the worst year of a whole people
a man set out from the workhouse with his wife.
He was walking – they were both walking – north.

She was sick with famine fever and could not keep up.
    He lifted her and put her on his back.
He walked like that west and west and north.
Until at nightfall under freezing stars they arrived.

In the morning they were both found dead.
    Of cold. Of hunger. Of the toxins of a whole history.
But her feet were held against his breastbone.
The last heat of his flesh was his last gift to her.

Let no love poem ever come to this threshold.
    There is no place here for the inexact
praise of the easy graces and sensuality of the body.
There is only time for this merciless inventory:

Their death together in the winter of 1847.
    Also what they suffered. How they lived.
And what there is between a man and woman.
And in which darkness it can best be proved.

EAVAN BOLAND (1944–2020)   159

FROM A SURVIVOR

The pact that we made was the ordinary pact
of men & women in those days

I don't know who we thought we were
that our personalities
could resist the failures of the race

Lucky or unlucky, we didn't know
the race had failures of that order
and that we were going to share them

Like everybody else, we thought of ourselves
        as special

Your body is as vivid to me
as it ever was: even more

since my feeling for it is clearer:
I know what it could and could not do

it is no longer
the body of a god
or anything with power over my life

Next year it would have been 20 years
and you are wastefully dead
who might have made the leap
we talked, too late, of making

which I live now
not as a leap
but a succession of brief, amazing movements

each one making possible the next

FOR CHIARA

Leaves crackle beneath our feet – tinder, kindling –
as we walk by the brook, the crab apple tree
a crimson pointillist nimbus.
You want to hold each wounded soul in your hands.
Autumn flares. The damaged, the human berserk,
find their way to you. I don't know how you sleep.
In the Gorgon's blood, one drop is poison, the other
     heals.
Fevered autumn, autumn I adore
croons an old song. We stroll the road
scuffing dust. And come upon
a garter snake lying motionless,
its tail, we guess, nicked by a passing car.
When we nudge it, it flips to its back in an agonized S,
squirms, but can't advance. Its belly gleams.
We edge it into the grass. Do we stop seeing
when we walk away? The brook prattles on.
Home's far off. Dusk settles, slowly, among leaves.
That's not mercy, scattering from its hands.

BLACK SILK

I see myself far off, in a mirror
        that has lost its shine.
                What time is it?
        What year? I stand, naked,
at the sink of a hotel room somewhere,

wringing a cloth. You lie on the bed.
        What are you watching?
                You know my body
        better than I, where it aches,
when it lied. A certain silken gleam:

from even further back, I remember
        a suture of railroad track
                trying to bind
        some siding of civilization
to a tumbleweed, as if that would hold.

It held, scar on my desert of a heart.
        Love, how many years till –
                an ocean away
        and no doctor at hand
in a strange country – you knelt over me

in a rented room and removed a few stitches
     from my skin? You showed
          the awkwardness of one
     who couldn't sew, the tenderness
of one who'd never ripped anything out.

MIRACLE

Not the one who takes up his bed and walks
But the ones who have known him all along
And carry him in —

Their shoulders numb, the ache and stoop deeplocked
In their backs, the stretcher handles
Slippery with sweat. And no let-up

Until he's strapped on tight, made tiltable
And raised to the tiled roof, then lowered for healing.
Be mindful of them as they stand and wait

For the burn of the paid-out ropes to cool,
Their slight lightheadedness and incredulity
To pass, those ones who had known him all along.

ON THE ASYLUM ROAD

Theirs is the house whose windows – every pane –
   Are made of darkly stained or clouded glass:
Sometimes you come upon them in the lane,
   The saddest crowd that you will ever pass.

But still we merry town or village folk
   Throw to their scattered stare a kindly grin,
And think no shame to stop and crack a joke
   With the incarnate wages of man's sin.

None but ourselves in our long gallery we meet,
   The moor-hen stepping from her reeds with dainty
      feet,
     The hare-bell bowing on his stem,
Dance not with us; their pulses beat
   To fainter music; nor do we to them
      Make their life sweet.

The gayest crowd that they will ever pass
   Are we to brother-shadows in the lane:
Our windows, too, are clouded glass
   To them, yes, every pane!

EVENING IN THE SANITARIUM

The free evening fades, outside the windows fastened
 with decorative iron grilles.
The lamps are lighted; the shades drawn; the nurses
 are watching a little.
It is the hour of the complicated knitting on the safe
 bone needles; of the games of anagrams and
 bridge;
The deadly game of chess; the book held up like a
 mask.

The period of the wildest weeping, the fiercest
 delusion, is over.
The women rest their tired half-healed hearts; they
 are almost well.
Some of them will stay almost well always: the blunt-
 faced woman whose thinking dissolved
Under academic discipline; the manic-depressive girl
Now leveling off; one paranoiac afflicted with jealousy.
Another with persecution. Some alleviation has been
 possible.

O fortunate bride, who never again will become elated
 after childbirth!
O lucky older wife, who has been cured of feeling
 unwanted!

To the suburban railway station you will return,
    return,
To meet forever Jim home on the 5:35.
You will be again as normal and selfish and heartless
    as anybody else.

There is life left: the piano says it with its octave
    smile.
The soft carpets pad the thump and splinter of the
    suicide to be.
Everything will be splendid: the grandmother will
    not drink habitually.
The fruit salad will bloom on the plate like a bouquet
And the garden produce the blue-ribbon aquilegia.

The cats will be glad; the fathers feel justified; the
    mothers relieved.
The sons and husbands will no longer need to pay the
    bills.
Childhoods will be put away, the obscene nightmare
    abated.

At the ends of the corridors the baths are running.
Mrs C. again feels the shadow of the obsessive idea.
Miss R. looks at the mantel-piece, which must mean
    something.

TULIPS

The tulips are too excitable, it is winter here.
Look how white everything is, how quiet, how
      snowed-in.
I am learning peacefulness, lying by myself quietly
As the light lies on these white walls, this bed, these
      hands.
I am nobody; I have nothing to do with explosions.
I have given my name and my day-clothes up to the
      nurses
And my history to the anesthetist and my body to
      surgeons.

They have propped my head between the pillow and
      the sheet-cuff
Like an eye between two white lids that will not shut.
Stupid pupil, it has to take everything in.
The nurses pass and pass, they are no trouble,
They pass the way gulls pass inland in their white
      caps,
Doing things with their hands, one just the same as
      another,
So it is impossible to tell how many there are.

My body is a pebble to them, they tend it as water
Tends to the pebbles it must run over, smoothing
     them gently.
They bring me numbness in their bright needles, they
     bring me sleep.
Now I have lost myself I am sick of baggage –
My patent leather overnight case like a black pillbox,
My husband and child smiling out of the family photo;
Their smiles catch onto my skin, little smiling hooks.

I have let things slip, a thirty-year-old cargo boat
Stubbornly hanging on to my name and address.
They have swabbed me clear of my loving
     associations.
Scared and bare on the green plastic-pillowed trolley
I watched my teaset, my bureaus of linen, my books
Sink out of sight, and the water went over my head.
I am a nun now, I have never been so pure.

I didn't want any flowers, I only wanted
To lie with my hands turned up and be utterly empty.
How free it is, you have no idea how free –
The peacefulness is so big it dazes you,
And it asks nothing, a name tag, a few trinkets.
It is what the dead close on, finally; I imagine them
Shutting their mouths on it, like a Communion tablet.

The tulips are too red in the first place, they hurt me.
Even through the gift paper I could hear them breathe
Lightly, through their white swaddlings, like an awful
     baby.
Their redness talks to my wound, it corresponds.
They are subtle: they seem to float, though they weigh
     me down,
Upsetting me with their sudden tongues and their
     color,
A dozen red lead sinkers round my neck.

Nobody watched me before, now I am watched.
The tulips turn to me, and the window behind me
Where once a day the light slowly widens and slowly
     thins,
And I see myself, flat, ridiculous, a cut-paper shadow
Between the eye of the sun and the eyes of the tulips,
And I have no face, I have wanted to efface myself.
The vivid tulips eat my oxygen.

Before they came the air was calm enough,
Coming and going, breath by breath, without any
     fuss.
Then the tulips filled it up like a loud noise.
Now the air snags and eddies round them the way
     a river
Snags and eddies round a sunken rust-red engine.

They concentrate my attention, that was happy
Playing and resting without committing itself.

The walls, also, seem to be warming themselves.
The tulips should be behind bars like dangerous
      animals;
They are opening like the mouth of some great
      African cat,
And I am aware of my heart: it opens and closes
Its bowl of red blooms out of sheer love of me.
The water I taste is warm and salt, like the sea,
And comes from a country far away as health.

HOME AFTER THREE MONTHS AWAY

Gone now the baby's nurse,
a lioness who ruled the roost
and made the Mother cry.
She used to tie
gobbets of porkrind in bowknots of gauze –
three months they hung like soggy toast
on our eight foot magnolia tree,
and helped the English sparrows
weather a Boston winter.

Three months, three months!
Is Richard now himself again?
Dimpled with exaltation,
my daughter holds her levee in the tub.
Our noses rub,
each of us pats a stringy lock of hair –
they tell me nothing's gone.
Though I am forty-one,
not forty now, the time I put away
was child's-play. After thirteen weeks
my child still dabs her cheeks
to start me shaving. When
we dress her in her sky-blue corduroy,
she changes to a boy,
and floats my shaving brush

and washcloth in the flush. . . .
Dearest, I cannot loiter here
in lather like a polar bear.

Recuperating, I neither spin nor toil.
Three stories down below,
a choreman tends our coffin's length of soil,
and seven horizontal tulips blow.
Just twelve months ago,
these flowers were pedigreed
imported Dutchmen; now no one need
distinguish them from weed.
Bushed by the late spring snow,
they cannot meet
another year's snowballing enervation.

I keep no rank nor station.
Cured, I am frizzled, stale and small.

"AFTER GREAT PAIN, A FORMAL FEELING COMES –"

After great pain, a formal feeling comes –
The Nerves sit ceremonious, like Tombs –
The stiff Heart questions was it He, that bore,
And Yesterday, or Centuries before?

The Feet, mechanical, go round –
Of Ground, or Air, or Ought –
A Wooden way
Regardless grown,
A Quartz contentment, like a stone –

This is the Hour of Lead –
Remembered, if outlived,
As Freezing persons, recollect the Snow –
First – Chill – then Stupor – then the letting go –

EMILY DICKINSON (1830–86)   175

MORNING GLORY

Out my window, in a garden the size of an urn,

a morning glory is climbing toward me.

It is five a.m. on the ninth day of the seventh month.

Lying on my soft mats, like a long white rabbit,

I can feel the purifying flames of summer

denuding the landscape, not of birds and animals,

but of blame and illusion. I can hear the white

splashing rivers of forgetfulness and oblivion

soaking me all at once, like loving a man

without wanting him, or a baby emerging

under white light out of its mother,

not the artificial light of the hospital corridor

but of joy growing wild in the garden, its pallid blue

trumpets piercing a brocade of red leaves.

CARRION COMFORT

Not, I'll not, carrion comfort, Despair, not feast on
    thee;
Not untwist – slack they may be – these last strands
    of man
In me ór, most weary, cry *I can no more.* I can;
Can something, hope, wish day come, not choose not
    to be.

But ah, but O thou terrible, why wouldst thou rude
    on me
Thy wring-world right foot rock? lay a lionlimb
    against me? scan
With darksome devouring eyes my bruisèd bones?
    and fan,
O in turns of tempest, me heaped there; me frantic to
    avoid thee and flee?

Why? That my chaff might fly; my grain lie, sheer
    and clear.
Nay in all that toil, that coil, since (seems) I kissed
    the rod,
Hand rather, my heart lo! lapped strength, stole joy,
    would laugh, chéer.
Cheer whom though? The hero whose heaven-
    handling flung me, fóot tród

Me? or me that fought him? O which one? is it each
    one? That night, that year
Of now done darkness I wretch lay wrestling with
    (my God!) my God.

From IN MEMORIAM

Be near me when my light is low,
 When the blood creeps, and the nerves prick
 And tingle; and the heart is sick,
And all the wheels of Being slow.

Be near me when the sensuous frame
 Is rack'd with pangs that conquer trust;
 And Time, a maniac scattering dust,
And Life, a Fury slinging flame.

Be near me when my faith is dry,
 And men the flies of latter spring,
 That lay their eggs, and sting and sing
And weave their petty cells and die.

Be near me when I fade away,
 To point the term of human strife,
 And on the low dark verge of life
The twilight of eternal day.

ALFRED, LORD TENNYSON (1809–92)   179

"THEY SAY THAT 'TIME ASSUAGES'–"

They say that "Time assuages" –
Time never did assuage –
An actual suffering strengthens
As Sinews do, with age –

Time is a Test of Trouble –
But not a Remedy –
If such it prove, it prove too
There was no Malady –

RETROACTIVE

If reward or
amends could
set the clock
back, as happens
in fall when
an hour is stalled
for the sake of light,
then our golgothas
could be put right.
The kiss or reform
or return of the
family farm would
soak into the
injury, ease the
knot of memory,
unname the site
of harm. If there
could be one day
– one hour – of jubilee
how many lame
would walk their property.

WHEN YOU HAVE FORGOTTEN SUNDAY:
THE LOVE STORY

—And when you have forgotten the bright bedclothes
    on a Wednesday and a Saturday,
And most especially when you have forgotten
    Sunday –
When you have forgotten Sunday halves in bed,
Or me sitting on the front-room radiator in the
    limping afternoon
Looking off down the long street
To nowhere,
Hugged by my plain old wrapper of no-expectation
And nothing-I-have-to-do and I'm-happy-why?
And if-Monday-never-had-to-come –
When you have forgotten that, I say,
And how you swore, if somebody beeped the bell,
And how my heart played hopscotch if the telephone
    rang;
And how we finally went in to Sunday dinner,
That is to say, went across the front room floor to the
    ink-spotted table in the southwest corner
To Sunday dinner, which was always chicken and
    noodles
Or chicken and rice
And salad and rye bread and tea
And chocolate chip cookies –

I say, when you have forgotten that,
When you have forgotten my little presentiment
That the war would be over before they got to you;
And how we finally undressed and whipped out the
     light and flowed into bed,
And lay loose-limbed for a moment in the week-end
Bright bedclothes,
Then gently folded into each other –
When you have, I say, forgotten all that,
Then you may tell,
Then I may believe
You have forgotten me well.

MITTELBERGHEIM

Wine sleeps in casks of Rhine oak.
I am wakened by the bell of a chapel in the vineyards
Of Mittelbergheim. I hear a small spring
Trickling into a well in the yard, a clatter
Of sabots in the street. Tobacco drying
Under the eaves, and ploughs and wooden wheels
And mountain slopes and autumn are with me.

I keep my eyes closed. Do not rush me,
You, fire, power, might, for it is too early.
I have lived through many years and, as in this
    half-dream,
I felt I was attaining the moving frontier
Beyond which color and sound come true
And the things of this earth are united.
Do not yet force me to open my lips.
Let me trust and believe I will attain.
Let me linger here in Mittelbergheim.

I know I should. They are with me,
Autumn and wooden wheels and tobacco hung
Under the eaves. Here and everywhere
Is my homeland, wherever I turn
And in whatever language I would hear
The song of a child, the conversation of lovers.

Happier than anyone, I am to receive
A glance, a smile, a star, silk creased
At the knee. Serene, beholding,
I am to walk on hills in the soft glow of day
Over waters, cities, roads, human customs.

Fire, power, might, you who hold me
In the palm of your hand whose furrows
Are like immense gorges combed
By southern wind. You who grant certainty
In the hour of fear, in the week of doubt,
It is too early, let the wine mature,
Let the travelers sleep in Mittelbergheim.

CZESŁAW MIŁOSZ (1911–2004)
TRANSLATED BY THE AUTHOR AND
RICHARD LOURIE

MY LADY'S GRAVE

The linnet in the rocky dells,
    The moor-lark in the air,
The bee among the heather bells
    That hide my lady fair:

The wild deer browse above her breast;
    The wild birds raise their brood;
And they, her smiles of love caress'd,
    Have left her solitude!

I ween that when the grave's dark wall
    Did first her form retain,
They thought their hearts could ne'er recall
    The light of joy again.

They thought the tide of grief would flow
    Uncheck'd through future years;
But where is all their anguish now,
    And where are all their tears?

Well, let them fight for honour's breath,
    Or pleasure's shade pursue –
The dweller in the land of death
    Is changed and careless too.

And if their eyes should watch and weep
    Till sorrow's source were dry,
She would not, in her tranquil sleep,
    Return a single sigh!

Blow, west wind, by the lonely mound:
    And murmur, summer streams!
There is no need of other sound
    To soothe my lady's dreams.

EMILY BRONTË (1818–48)

REMEMBER

Remember me when I am gone away,
   Gone far away into the silent land;
   When you can no more hold me by the hand,
Nor I half turn to go yet turning stay.
Remember me when no more, day by day,
   You tell me of our future that you planned:
   Only remember me; you understand
It will be late to counsel then or pray.
Yet if you should forget me for a while
   And afterwards remember, do not grieve:
   For if the darkness and corruption leave
   A vestige of the thoughts that once I had,
Better by far you should forget and smile
   Than that you should remember and be sad.

SONNET XXIII

Methought I saw my late espousèd Saint
    Brought to me like *Alcestis* from the grave,
    Whom *Jove's* great Son to her glad Husband gave,
    Rescu'd from death by force though pale and faint.
Mine as whom washt from spot of child-bed taint,
    Purification in the old Law did save,
    And such, as yet once more I trust to have
    Full sight of her in Heaven without restraint,
Came vested all in white, pure as her mind:
    Her face was veil'd, yet to my fancied sight,
    Love, sweetness, goodness, in her person shin'd
So clear, as in no face with more delight.
    But O, as to embrace me she inclin'd,
    I wak'd, she fled, and day brought back my night.

THE HOUSE

Sometimes, on waking, she would close her eyes
For a last look at that white house she knew
In sleep alone, and held no title to,
And had not entered yet, for all her sighs.

What did she tell me of that house of hers?
White gatepost; terrace; fanlight of the door;
A widow's walk above the bouldered shore;
Salt winds that ruffle the surrounding firs.

Is she now there, wherever there may be?
Only a foolish man would hope to find
That haven fashioned by her dreaming mind.
Night after night, my love, I put to sea.

THE CROSS OF SNOW

In the long, sleepless watches of the night,
    A gentle face – the face of one long dead –
    Looks at me from the wall, where round its head
    The night-lamp casts a halo of pale light.
Here in this room she died; and soul more white
    Never through martyrdom of fire was led
    To its repose; nor can in books be read
    The legend of a life more benedight.
There is a mountain in the distant West
    That, sun-defying, in its deep ravines
    Displays a cross of snow upon its side.
Such is the cross I wear upon my breast
    These eighteen years, through all the changing
        scenes
    And seasons, changeless since the day she died.

"TOMORROW AS SOON AS THE COUNTRYSIDE PALES WITH DAWN"

Tomorrow as soon as the countryside pales with
    dawn,
    I will leave. You see, I know you are waiting.
    I do.
I will travel through the forest, I will travel through
    the mountain.
    I cannot any longer stay far away from you.

I will walk with my own thought the focus of my
    gaze,
    seeing nothing outside, not hearing it,
alone, unknown, with a stooped back and hands that
    cross,
    sad, and the day for me will be like night.

I will not look for evening's falling gold to come,
    nor the distant sails on a reach for Honfleur,
and when I get there I will lay on your tomb
    a bunch of green holly and one of blooming
    heather.

192   VICTOR HUGO (1802–85)
    TRANSLATED BY KARL KIRCHWEY

THE KALEIDOSCOPE

To climb these stairs again, bearing a tray,
Might be to find you pillowed with your books,
Your inventories listing gowns and frocks
As if preparing for a holiday.
Or, turning from the landing, I might find
My presence watched through your kaleidoscope,
A symmetry of husbands, each redesigned
In lovely forms of foresight, prayer and hope.
I climb these stairs a dozen times a day
And, by that open door, wait, looking in
At where you died. My hands become a tray
Offering me, my flesh, my soul, my skin.
Grief wrongs us so. I stand, and wait, and cry
For the absurd forgiveness, not knowing why.

From LONG DISTANCE

Though my mother was already two years dead
Dad kept her slippers warming by the gas,
put hot water bottles her side of the bed
and still went to renew her transport pass.

You couldn't just drop in. You had to phone.
He'd put you off an hour to give him time
to clear away her things and look alone
as though his still raw love were such a crime.

He couldn't risk my blight of disbelief
though sure that very soon he'd hear her key
scrape in the rusted lock and end his grief.
He *knew* she'd just popped out to get the tea.

I believe life ends with death, and that is all.
You haven't both gone shopping; just the same,
in my new black leather phone book there's your name
and the disconnected number I still call.

CELEBRATION

Seeing, in April, hostas unfurl like arias,
and tulips, white cups inscribed with licks of flame,
gaze feverish, grown almost to my waist,
and the oaks raise new leaves for benediction,
I mourn for what does not come back: the movie
    theater –
reels spinning out vampire bats, last trains,
the arc of Chaplin's cane, the hidden doorways –
struck down for a fast-food store; your rangy stride;
my shawl of hair; my mother's grand piano.
My mother.

                How to make it new,
how to find the gain in it? Ask the sea
at sunrise how a million sparks
can fly over dead bones.

FAREWELL PERFORMANCE
for DK

Art. It cures affliction. As lights go down and
Maestro lifts his wand, the unfailing sea change
starts within us. Limber alembics once more
make of the common

lot a pure, brief gold. At the end our bravos
call them back, sweat-soldered and leotarded,
back, again back – anything not to face the
fact that it's over.

You are gone. You'd caught like a cold their airy
lust for essence. Now, in the furnace parched to
ten or twelve light handfuls, a mortal gravel
sifted through fingers,

coarse yet grayly glimmering sublimate of
palace days, Strauss, Sidney, the lover's plaintive
Can't we just be friends? which your breakfast phone call
clothed in amusement,

this is what we paddled a neighbor's dinghy
out to scatter – Peter who grasped the buoy,
I who held the box underwater, freeing
all it contained. Past

sunny, fluent soundings that gruel of selfhood
taking manlike shape for one last jeté on
ghostly – wait, ah! – point into darkness vanished.
High up, a gull's wings

clapped. The house lights (always supposing, caro,
Earth remains your house) at their brightest set the
scene for good: true colors, the sun-warm hand to
cover my wet one. . . .

Back they come. How you would have loved it. We in
turn have risen. Pity and terror done with,
programs furled, lips parted, we jostle forward
eager to hail them,

more, to join the troupe – will a friend enroll us
one fine day? Strange, though. For up close their
        magic
self-destructs. Pale, dripping, with downcast eyes
        they've
seen where it led you.

CAT IN AN EMPTY APARTMENT

Die – you can't do that to a cat.
Since what can a cat do
in an empty apartment?
Climb the walls?
Rub up against the furniture?
Nothing seems different here,
but nothing is the same.
Nothing has been moved,
but there's more space.
And at nighttime no lamps are lit.

Footsteps on the staircase,
but they're new ones.
The hand that puts fish on the saucer
has changed, too.

Something doesn't start
at its usual time.
Something doesn't happen
as it should.
Someone was always, always here,
then suddenly disappeared
and stubbornly stays disappeared.

Every closet has been examined.
Every shelf has been explored.
Excavations under the carpet turned up nothing.
A commandment was even broken:
papers scattered everywhere.
What remains to be done.
Just sleep and wait.

Just wait till he turns up,
just let him show his face.
Will he ever get a lesson
on what not to do to a cat.
Sidle toward him
as if unwilling
and ever so slow
on visibly offended paws,
and no leaps or squeals at least to start.

WISŁAWA SZYMBORSKA (1923–2012) 199
TRANSLATED BY STANISŁAW BARAŃCZAK
AND CLARE CAVANAGH

TALKING TO MYSELF
(*for Oliver Sacks*)

Spring this year in Austria started off benign,
the heavens lucid, the air stable, the about
sane to all feeders, vegetate or bestial:
the deathless minerals looked pleased with their regime,
where what is not forbidden is compulsory.

Shadows of course there are, Porn-Ads, with-it clergy,
and hubby next door has taken to the bottle,
but You have preserved Your poise, strange rustic
    object,
whom I, made in God's Image but already warped,
a malapert will-worship, must bow to as Me.

My mortal manor, the carnal territory
allotted to my manage, my fosterling too,
I must earn cash to support, my tutor also,
but for whose neural instructions I could never
acknowledge what is or imagine what is not.

Instinctively passive, I guess, having neither
fangs nor talons nor hooves nor venom, and therefore
too prone to let the sun go down upon Your funk,
a poor smeller, or rather a censor of smells,
with an omnivore palate that can take hot food.

Unpredictably, decades ago, You arrived
among that unending cascade of creatures spewed
from Nature's maw. A random event, says Science.
Random my bottom! A true miracle, say I,
for who is not certain that he was meant to be?

As You augmented and developed a profile,
I looked at Your looks askance. *His architecture
should have been much more imposing: I've been let down!*
By now, though, I've gotten used to Your proportions
and, all things considered, I might have fared
    far worse.

Seldom have You been a bother. For many years
You were, I admit, a martyr to horn-colic
(it did no good to tell You – *But I'm not in love!*):
how stoutly, though, You've repelled all germ
    invasions,
but never chastised my tantrums with a megrim.

You are the Injured Party for, if short-sighted,
I am the book-worm who tired You, if short-winded
as cigarette addicts are, I was the pusher
who got You hooked. (Had we been both a bit
    younger,
I might well have mischiefed You worse with
    a needle.)

I'm always amazed at how little I know You.
Your coasts and outgates I know, for I govern there,
but what goes on inland, the rites, the social codes,
Your torrents, salt and sunless, remain enigmas:
what I believe is on doctors' hearsay only.

Our marriage is a drama, but no stage-play where
what is not spoken is not thought: in our theatre
all that I cannot syllable You will pronounce
in acts whose *raison-d'être* escapes me. Why secrete
fluid when I dole, or stretch Your lips when I joy?

Demands to close or open, include or eject,
must come from Your corner, are no province of mine
(all I have done is to provide the time-table
of hours when You may put them): but what is
     Your work
when I librate between a glum and a frolic?

For dreams I, quite irrationally, reproach You.
All I know is that I don't choose them: if I could,
they would conform to some prosodic discipline,
mean just what they say. Whatever point nocturnal
manias make, as a poet I disapprove.

Thanks to Your otherness, Your jocular concords,
so unlike my realm of dissonance and anger,
You can serve me as my emblem for the Cosmos:
for human congregations, though, as Hobbes
    perceived,
the apposite sign is some ungainly monster.

Whoever coined the phrase *The Body Politic*?
All States we've lived in, or historians tell of,
have had shocking health, psychosomatic cases,
physicked by sadists or glozing expensive quacks:
when I read the papers, You seem an Adonis.

Time, we both know, will decay You, and already
I'm scared of our divorce: I've seen some horrid ones.
Remember: when *Le Bon Dieu* says to You *Leave him!*,
please, please, for His sake and mine, pay no attention
to my piteous *Don'ts*, but bugger off quickly.

THE WOUND

The huge wound in my head began to heal
About the beginning of the seventh week.
Its valleys darkened, its villages became still:
For joy I did not move and dared not speak,
Not doctors would cure it, but time, its patient skill.

And constantly my mind returned to Troy.
After I sailed the seas I fought in turn
On both sides, sharing even Helen's joy
Of place, and growing up – to see Troy burn –
As Neoptolemus, that stubborn boy.

I lay and rested as prescription said.
Manoeuvered with the Greeks, or sallied out
Each day with Hector. Finally my bed
Became Achilles' tent, to which the lout
Thersites came reporting numbers dead.

I was myself: subject to no man's breath:
My own commander was my enemy.
And while my belt hung up, sword in the sheath,
Thersites shambled in and breathlessly
Cackled about my friend Patroclus' death.

I called for armour, rose, and did not reel.
But, when I thought, rage at his noble pain
Flew to my head, and turning I could feel
My wound break open wide. Over again
I had to let those storm-lit valleys heal.

TO MY DISSECTOR

I have not had a thought in years
So take this as you will.
When the blade slips into my chest
Blood doesn't hurry.

You are the one who feels it. We who are dead
Get a donation of feeling,
like coins tossed into a basket
At church. Who knows
Where they go after that?
The gifts are for the giver,
Specifically, for a little morose man in the giver's
     mind
Whom we will call Charon.

A consolation for Charon!
Watching trees sink as the river rises.
A heron's leg pierces the grey mirror.

NOTES FROM THE OTHER SIDE

I divested myself of despair
and fear when I came here.

Now there is no more catching
one's own eye in the mirror,

there are no bad books, no plastic,
no insurance premiums, and of course

no illness. Contrition
does not exist, nor gnashing

of teeth. No one howls as the first
clod of earth hits the casket.

The poor we no longer have with us.
Our calm hearts strike only the hour,

and God, as promised, proves
to be mercy clothed in light.

JANE KENYON (1947–95)   207

THE LOVER
After Propertius

Poor mortals, with your horoscopes and blood-tests –
what hope is there for you? Even if the plane
lands you safely, why should you not return
to your home in flames or ruins, your wife absconded,
the children blind and dying in their cots?
Even sitting quiet in a locked room
the perils are infinite and unforeseeable.
Only the lover walks upon the earth
careless of what the fates prepare for him:

so you step out at the lights, almost as if
you half-know that today you are the special one.
The woman in the windshield lifting away
her frozen cry, a white mask on a stick,
reveals herself as grey-eyed Atropos;
the sun leaves like a rocket; the sky goes out;
the road floods and widens; on the distant kerb
the lost souls groan and mew like sad trombones;
the ambulance glides up with its black sail –

when somewhere in the other world, she fills
your name full of her breath again, and at once
you float to your feet: the dark rose on your shirt
folds itself away, and you slip back

into the crowd, who, being merely human,
must remember nothing of this incident.
Just one flea-ridden dog chained to the railings,
who might be Cerberus, or patient Argos,
looks on, knowing the great law you have flouted.

CRUSH SYNDROME

Once when, in winter dark,
I was cleaning the concrete mixer,
its cogwheels, like the teeth
of a bored rat of Ibadan,
snapped up the glove
with the hand inside. The finger bones
said a few things you don't hear very often
and then it grew quiet, because
even the rat had panicked.

In that moment
I realized I had a soul.
It was soft, with red stripes,
and it wanted to be wrapped in gauze.
I put it beside me on the seat
and steered with the healthy hand. At the clinic,
during the injections of local anesthetic
and the stitching,
the soul held firmly with its mandibles
to the stainless steel knob of the adjustable table.
It was now whitish crystal
and had a grasshopper's head.

The fingers healed.
The soul turned, at first,
to granulation tissue,
and later a scar, scarcely visible.

MIROSLAV HOLUB (1923–98)

211

TRANSLATED BY DAVID YOUNG
AND DANA HÁBOVÁ

FACING IT

My black face fades,
hiding inside the black granite.
I said I wouldn't
dammit: No tears.
I'm stone. I'm flesh.
My clouded reflection eyes me
like a bird of prey, the profile of night
slanted against morning. I turn
this way – the stone lets me go.
I turn that way – I'm inside
the Vietnam Veterans Memorial
again, depending on the light
to make a difference.
I go down the 58,022 names,
half-expecting to find
my own in letters like smoke.
I touch the name Andrew Johnson;
I see the booby trap's white flash.
Names shimmer on a woman's blouse
but when she walks away
the names stay on the wall.
Brushstrokes flash, a red bird's
wings cutting across my stare.
The sky. A plane in the sky.
A white vet's image floats

212

closer to me, then his pale eyes
look through mine. I'm a window.
He's lost his right arm
inside the stone. In the black mirror
a woman's trying to erase names:
No, she's brushing a boy's hair.

CHORUS FROM *THE CURE AT TROY*

Human beings suffer,
They torture one another,
They get hurt and get hard.
No poem or play or song
Can fully right a wrong
Inflicted and endured.

The innocent in gaols
Beat on their bars together.
A hunger-striker's father
Stands in the graveyard dumb.
The police widow in veils
Faints at the funeral home.

History says, *Don't hope
On this side of the grave.*
But then, once in a lifetime
The longed-for tidal wave
Of justice can rise up,
And hope and history rhyme.

So hope for a great sea-change
On the far side of revenge.
Believe that a further shore
Is reachable from here.

Believe in miracles
And cures and healing wells.

Call miracle self-healing:
The utter, self-revealing
Double-take of feeling.
If there's fire on the mountain
Or lightning and storm
And a god speaks from the sky

That means someone is hearing
The outcry and the birth-cry
Of new life at its term.

MOLECULES

Whether it's true or not, that all our
molecules replace themselves each seven
years, his body seems halfway new again,
one year into sobriety. I keep my distance now
but recall his painful, ten-pound freight, the torpor
of late-term pregnancy. All those final weeks, I rested,
famished, calling for food I could spin into blood
and bones so he could thrive. Even then, his cravings
ruled us both – mindlessly, he craved to grow,
taking what he needed from my willing body
as – two decades later – he would steal
what he needed from my dresser drawers –
bank book, string of pearls, his grandmother's
tiny chip of diamond-studded wedding ring.
The latter must have brought him almost nothing
at the Cash for Gold store where all the junkies
        hang out.

HE STOOD THERE

When the gates of the hospital opened before him
and he went out into the street free
to go on his way, he stood there by the hospital gates
wondering whether to hail a taxi or to keep
walking, going out not coming in.

The avenue was already decorated for
Christmas, bathed in fluorescent light, a feat
of color, and the city lay open before him in all
directions and he wondered which way,
going out not coming in.

On the corner of Sixty-eighth Street, right opposite
the hospital, a Korean was selling all kinds
of novelties from his stall, including
masks at ninety cents each, and he stood there
wondering, going out
not coming in.

And when the policewoman blew her whistle,
to his surprise it sounded like the scream of a bird
shot by mistake, and he just turned his head
sideways and covered
half his face with a scarf
of wool.

Wool is not good, he thought,
it burns the skin, which is swollen like
the skin of a drum! And here he covered
his disfigurement with a splayed hand, striding
for the heart of the powerful wave that flowed
up the avenue bathed in lights, twinkling
for Christmas: Keep walking!
Keep walking! he said with locked
throat, in front of
the red
traffic light.

ABBA KOVNER (1918–87)
TRANSLATED BY EDDIE LEVENSTON

DISCHARGE

Winter & waiting over, the sun
melting snow on York Avenue
where a smile saying *We won*
can stop a cab. Released into

city streets littered with green
plastic tributes to St Patrick,
into midday traffic, into spring.
Medics going on a lunch break

flirting under the clockhand's
quivering supervision, a bell
next door on the Dominicans'
dispersing the shrieking gulls.

The river's steel waves scissor
& flash alongside FDR Drive;
we turn & lean into each other,
drunk on a sudden pour of time.

LITTLE PRAYER

let ruin end here

let him find honey
where there was once a slaughter

let him enter the lion's cage
& find a field of lilacs

let this be the healing
& if not   let it be

THE FLOWER

How fresh, O Lord, how sweet and clean
Are thy returns! ev'n as the flowers in spring;
To which, besides their own demean,
The late-past frosts tributes of pleasure bring.
Grief melts away
Like snow in May,
As if there were no such cold thing.

Who would have thought my shrivelled heart
Could have recovered greenness? It was gone
Quite underground; as flowers depart
To see their mother-root, when they have blown;
Where they together
All the hard weather,
Dead to the world, keep house unknown.

These are thy wonders, Lord of power,
Killing and quick'ning, bringing down to hell
And up to heaven in an hour;
Making a chiming of a passing-bell.
We say amiss,
This or that is:
Thy word is all, if we could spell.

O that I once past changing were,
Fast in thy Paradise, where no flower can wither!
   Many a spring I shoot up fair,
Off'ring at heav'n, growing and groaning thither:
        Nor doth my flower
        Want a spring-shower,
   My sins and I joining together:

   But while I grow in a straight line,
Still upwards bent, as if heav'n were mine own,
   Thy anger comes, and I decline:
What frost to that? what pole is not the zone,
        Where all things burn,
        When thou dost turn,
   And the least frown of thine is shown?

   And now in age I bud again,
After so many deaths I live and write;
   I once more smell the dew and rain,
And relish versing: O my only light,
        It cannot be
        That I am he
   On whom thy tempests fell all night.

These are thy wonders, Lord of love,
To make us see we are but flowers that glide:
Which when we once can find and prove,
Thou hast a garden for us, where to bide.
Who would be more,
Swelling through store,
Forfeit their Paradise by their pride.

SPRING

A window glimmering in wheeltracked clay
and someone skipping on the windowsill;
spins of her skipping-rope widen away.
She is dancing light and water
out of the cold side of the hill
and I've brought rhyme to meet her;
rhyme has been ill.

THE SUN THIS MARCH

The exceeding brightness of this early sun
Makes me conceive how dark I have become,

And re-illumines things that used to turn
To gold in broadest blue, and be a part

Of a turning spirit in an earlier self.
That, too, returns from out the winter's air,

Like an hallucination come to daze
The corner of the eye. Our element,

Cold is our element and winter's air
Brings voices as of lions coming down.

Oh! Rabbi, rabbi, fend my soul for me
And true savant of this dark nature be.

WALLACE STEVENS (1879 – 1955)   225

EVERYTHING IS GOING TO BE
ALL RIGHT

How should I not be glad to contemplate
the clouds clearing beyond the dormer window
and a high tide reflected on the ceiling?
There will be dying, there will be dying,
but there is no need to go into that.
The poems flow from the hand unbidden
and the hidden source is the watchful heart.
The sun rises in spite of everything
and the far cities are beautiful and bright.
I lie here in a riot of sunlight
watching the day break and the clouds flying.
Everything is going to be all right.

THE AMEN STONE

On my desk there is a stone with the word "Amen"
    on it,
a triangular fragment of stone from a Jewish graveyard
    destroyed
many generations ago. The other fragments, hundreds
    upon hundreds,
were scattered helter-skelter, and a great yearning,
a longing without end, fills them all:
first name in search of family name, date of death seeks
dead man's birthplace, son's name wishes to locate
name of father, date of birth seeks reunion with soul
that wishes to rest in peace. And until they have found
one another, they will not find perfect rest.
Only this stone lies calmly on my desk and says
    "Amen."
But now the fragments are gathered up in
    lovingkindness
by a sad good man. He cleanses them of every blemish,
photographs them one by one, arranges them on the
    floor
in the great hall, makes each gravestone whole again,
one again: fragment to fragment,
like the resurrection of the dead, a mosaic,
a jigsaw puzzle. Child's play.

YEHUDA AMICHAI (1924–2000)   227
TRANSLATED BY CHANA BLOCH AND
CHANA KRONFELD

O HEART, SMALL URN

O Heart, small urn
of porphyry, agate or cornelian,

how imperceptibly the grain fell
between a heart-beat of pleasure

and a heart-beat of pain;
I do not know how it came

nor how long it had lain there,
nor can I say

how it escaped tempest
of passion and malice,

nor why it was not washed away
in flood of sorrow,

or dried up in the bleak drought
of bitter thought.

H. D. (HILDA DOOLITTLE) (1886–1931)

NOT FOR THAT CITY

Not for that city of the level sun,
      Its golden streets and glittering gates ablaze –
      The shadeless, sleepless city of white days,
White nights, or nights and days that are as one –
We weary, when all is said, all thought, all done.
      We strain our eyes beyond this dusk to see
      What, from the threshold of eternity
We shall step into. No, I think we shun
The splendour of that everlasting glare,
      The clamour of that never-ending song.
      And if for anything we greatly long,
It is for some remote and quiet stair
      Which winds to silence and a space of sleep
      Too sound for waking, and for dreams
         too deep.

CHARLOTTE MEW (1869–1928)   229

From THE SECOND SERMON ON THE WARPLAND

Salve salvage in the spin.
Endorse the splendor splashes;
stylize the flawed utility;
prop a malign or failing light –
but know the whirlwind is our commonwealth.
Not the easy man, who rides above them all,
not the jumbo brigand,
not the pet bird of poets, that sweetest sonnet,
shall straddle the whirlwind.
Nevertheless, live.

ACKNOWLEDGMENTS

Thanks are due to the following copyright holders for permission to reprint:

JULIA ALVAREZ: "Are we all ill with acute loneliness" from *Homecoming* (1984). Susan Bergholz Literary Services. YEHUDA AMICHAI: "The Amen Stone" from *Open Closed Open: Poems* by Yehuda Amichai, translated from the Hebrew by Chana Bloch and Chana Kronfeld. Copyright © 2000 by Chana Bloch and Chana Kronfeld. Reprinted by permission of Houghton Mifflin Harcourt. All rights reserved. "The Amen Stone" (translated by Chana Bloch and Chana Kronfeld) from *Open Closed Open: Poems*, Georges Borchardt Agency. MARGARET ATWOOD: "Up" from *Morning in the Burned House: New Poems* by Margaret Atwood. Reprinted by permission of Houghton Mifflin Harcourt Publishing Company. All rights reserved. Oxford University Press, 1995. W. H. AUDEN: "Miss Gee", copyright 1940 and © renewed 1968 by W. H. Auden; and "Talking to Myself", copyright © 1972 by W. H. Auden; from *Collected Poems* by W. H. Auden, edited by Edward Mendelson. Used by permission of Random House, an imprint and division of Penguin Random House LLC. All rights reserved. Curtis Brown. CHARLES BAUDELAIRE: "Spleen (IV)" from *Les Fleurs du Mal*, translated by Richard Howard. English translation copyright © 1982 by Richard Howard. Reprinted with the permission of The Permissions Company, LLC on behalf of David R. Godine, Publisher, Inc., www. godine.com. "Invitation to the Voyage" (translated by Richard Wilbur) from *The Flowers of Evil*, ed. Jackson Mathews and Marthiel Mathews, New Directions, 1989. LOUISE BOGAN: "Evening in the Sanitarium" from *The Blue Estuaries: Poems*

237